PRAISE FOR ALFRED GIBSON

From "Wilderness Survival Hacks"

This comprehensive guide is a must-have for anyone interested in wilderness survival ... Having thru-hiked the Pacific Crest Trail the insights in this book are a must for those venturing into the outdoors.

— TONY & ALISA DILORENZO

... Clear explanations that were simple and easy to understand. Good recaps to make sure you remember what you had just learned ... comprehensive overview of all areas of basic survival skills.

— DOUGLAS MARK OLSEN

WILDERNESS LIFELINE

WILDERNESS LIFELINE

BUSHCRAFT FIRST AID FOR ULTIMATE SURVIVAL

WILDERNESS MASTERY ESSENTIALS
BOOK 2

ALFRED GIBSON

Copyright © 2024 by Alfred Gibson

All rights reserved. No part of this book may be reproduced, stored in a retrieval system, or transmitted in any form or by any means, electronic, mechanical, photocopying, recording, or otherwise, without the prior written permission of the publisher, Book Bound Studios.

The information contained in this book is based on the author's personal experiences and research. While every effort has been made to ensure the accuracy of the information presented, the author and publisher cannot be held responsible for any errors or omissions.

This book is intended for general informational purposes only and is not a substitute for professional medical, legal, or financial advice. If you have specific questions about any medical, legal, or financial matters, you should consult with a qualified healthcare professional, attorney, or financial advisor.

Book Bound Studios is not affiliated with any product or vendor mentioned in this book. The views expressed in this book are those of the author and do not necessarily reflect the views of Book Bound Studios.

To the untamed spirit of adventure in all of us and to the wilderness that both challenges and nurtures that spirit. This book is dedicated to the brave souls who seek to understand and respect the natural world and to my family, who has always supported my wild pursuits. May this guide serve as a bridge between the ancient wisdom of the earth and the modern seekers of adventure, ensuring safe passage through the wild for generations to come.

Between every two pines is a doorway to a new world.

— JOHN MUIR

CONTENTS

Introduction to Bushcraft First Aid   xv

1. BASIC FIRST AID SKILLS   1
   Performing CPR in the Wilderness   1
   Dealing with Bleeding and Wounds   4
   Managing Sprains and Fractures   6
   Recognizing and Treating Hypothermia and Heatstroke   8
   Creating and Using Splints from Natural Materials   11
   Chapter Summary   13

2. NATURAL REMEDIES AND PLANT MEDICINE   17
   Identifying Medicinal Plants   17
   Preparing Poultices and Salves   20
   Natural Antiseptics in the Wild   23
   Using Herbs for Pain Relief   25
   The Role of Nutrition in Healing   28
   Chapter Summary   31

3. HANDLING ANIMAL AND INSECT BITES   33
   Identifying Dangerous Animals and Insects   33
   First Aid for Snake Bites   36
   Treating Insect Stings and Bites   38
   Preventing and Treating Tick Bites   40
   Rabies Prevention and First Response   42
   Chapter Summary   45

4. WATER SAFETY AND HYDRATION — 47
- Finding and Purifying Water — 47
- Recognizing Signs of Dehydration — 49
- Treating Waterborne Illnesses — 52
- Safe Swimming Practices — 54
- Chapter Summary — 56

5. FOOD SAFETY AND NUTRITION — 59
- Foraging for Edible Plants — 59
- Hunting and Fishing for Survival — 62
- Preventing Foodborne Illnesses — 64
- Cooking and Preserving Wild Food — 66
- Chapter Summary — 68

6. SHELTER AND EXPOSURE PROTECTION — 71
- Choosing a Safe Shelter Location — 71
- Building Insulated Shelters — 74
- Protecting Yourself from the Elements — 76
- Fire Safety and Warmth — 78
- Chapter Summary — 81

7. NAVIGATING MENTAL HEALTH CHALLENGES — 83
- Coping with Stress and Anxiety — 83
- The Psychological Impact of Survival Situations — 86
- Building Resilience and Mental Toughness — 89
- Chapter Summary — 91

8. EMERGENCY SIGNALING AND RESCUE — 93
- Creating Effective Signals — 93
- Using Technology for Rescue — 96
- Navigational Aids and Techniques — 98
- Interacting with Rescuers — 101

Preparing for Evacuation	103
Chapter Summary	106

9. WEATHER AND ENVIRONMENTAL HAZARDS — 109

Understanding Weather Patterns	109
Preparing for Extreme Weather Conditions	112
Avoiding Natural Hazards	115
Surviving in Different Climates	117
Minimizing Environmental Impact	119
Chapter Summary	122

10. ADVANCED FIRST AID TECHNIQUES — 125

Suturing Wounds in the Field	125
Managing Severe Allergic Reactions	128
Field Management of Dental Emergencies	131
Handling Psychological First Aid	133
Evacuation and Long-Term Care Planning	136
Chapter Summary	139
The Journey Ahead	141
Your Feedback Matters	155
About the Author	157

INTRODUCTION TO BUSHCRAFT FIRST AID

A medical kit on a bench in the wilderness.

Understanding the Basics of Bushcraft

Bushcraft, at its core, is the skill set required to thrive in the natural environment. It encompasses a broad range

Introduction to Bushcraft First Aid

of knowledge, from identifying edible plants and navigating the wilderness to creating shelters and managing fire. However, first aid is one aspect of bushcraft that is often overlooked yet equally vital. Understanding the basics of bushcraft is not just about mastering the environment; it's also about knowing how to respond to the challenges and emergencies that may arise within it.

First aid knowledge becomes indispensable in the wild for several reasons. The isolation and often remote locations mean that medical help could be away for hours if not days. In such scenarios, the ability to administer first aid can make a significant difference in the outcome of an emergency. This could range from treating minor cuts and burns to managing more severe conditions like hypothermia or heatstroke until professional help can be reached.

Moreover, the wilderness presents unique challenges and hazards not commonly encountered in urban settings. The variety of potential emergencies is vast, from insect bites and animal attacks to injuries from tools and natural elements. A solid understanding of first aid allows bushcraft enthusiasts to prepare for and respond to these specific challenges effectively. It's not just about applying a bandage; it's about knowing how to adapt and use the resources available in nature

Introduction to Bushcraft First Aid

to aid in treatment. For instance, knowing which plants have antiseptic properties or how to create a splint using branches could be life-saving.

In addition to treating injuries and illnesses, first aid knowledge encompasses prevention. Understanding how to avoid common hazards, recognizing the signs of severe conditions like dehydration or frostbite, and knowing when to seek shelter can prevent emergencies from occurring in the first place. This proactive approach to health and safety is fundamental to bushcraft, ensuring that adventurers can enjoy the wilderness while minimizing risks.

First aid is a critical component of bushcraft that complements and enhances the traditional skills associated with wilderness survival. It empowers individuals to survive and do so safely, with a well-rounded understanding of how to care for themselves and others in the natural environment. As we delve deeper into the specifics of bushcraft first aid in the following sections, we will explore the practical skills and knowledge necessary to handle a wide range of situations, ensuring that enthusiasts are well-prepared for their adventures in the wild.

Introduction to Bushcraft First Aid

The Importance of First Aid Knowledge in the Wild

Venturing into the wilderness, whether for leisure or as a part of a lifestyle choice, brings with it an unparalleled sense of freedom and connection to nature. However, this adventure also exposes one to various risks and potential emergencies that can arise from the unpredictable elements of the wild. In this context, the knowledge of first aid becomes not just functional but essential. The ability to respond effectively to injuries or health issues when professional medical help is not immediately accessible can mean the difference between a minor setback and a life-threatening situation.

First aid knowledge equips you with the skills to assess and manage minor and major emergencies, from treating cuts, burns, and bites to addressing more serious concerns such as hypothermia, heatstroke, or severe allergic reactions. Understanding how to stabilize a patient until professional medical help can be reached is a critical skill set that can save lives. This is especially true in bushcraft and wilderness settings where the nearest help could be hours, if not days, away.

Moreover, being proficient in first aid instills

Introduction to Bushcraft First Aid

confidence and calmness in handling emergencies, which can be contagious and help keep others calm. It also fosters a proactive approach to safety, encouraging the preparation and prevention mindset that is crucial in bushcraft. Knowing how to avoid common hazards and minimize risks through proper preparation and awareness can prevent many emergencies from occurring in the first place.

In addition to dealing with emergencies, first aid knowledge is also about maintaining one's health in the wilderness. This includes knowledge about hydration, nutrition, and the prevention of common ailments that can occur in outdoor settings. It's about making informed decisions regarding your well-being and that of your companions, ensuring that the wilderness experience remains safe and enjoyable for everyone involved.

As we delve deeper into the specifics of bushcraft first aid in the following sections, it's important to remember that this knowledge is not just about dealing with emergencies. It's also about enhancing our connection with the natural world through a deeper understanding of caring for ourselves and others in the wilderness. With this foundation, we can approach our adventures with greater confidence, respect for the wild, and a commitment to safety that ensures our experiences are enjoyable but also responsible and sustainable.

Preparing Your First Aid Kit

Having established the foundational importance of first aid knowledge in the wilderness, let's discuss preparing your first aid kit. This kit is your frontline defense against minor injuries. It could be the difference between a minor inconvenience and a major emergency. The contents of your kit should be meticulously selected to cater to the unique challenges and risks associated with bushcraft activities.

First and foremost, your kit should include a variety of bandages. This includes adhesive bandages of various sizes for minor cuts and scrapes, sterile gauze pads for larger wounds, and elastic bandages for sprains or strains. It's also wise to include a roll of medical tape to secure gauze in place.

Antiseptic wipes and antibiotic ointments are crucial for cleaning and protecting wounds from infection. The risk of infection in the wilderness is heightened due to exposure to the elements and potentially unclean conditions. Therefore, ensuring wounds are correctly cleaned and dressed is paramount.

In addition to wound care supplies, your kit should

contain items to address other common ailments and injuries. This includes antihistamines for allergic reactions, pain relievers such as ibuprofen or acetaminophen, and anti-diarrheal medications. Given the nature of bushcraft activities, including a tick removal tool and insect sting relief treatment is also prudent.

A critical but often overlooked component is a pair of medical-grade gloves. These serve two essential purposes: protecting the caregiver from potential bloodborne pathogens and keeping the treatment area as sterile as possible.

A CPR mask and tourniquet can be lifesaving for more severe emergencies. While these items require proper practical training, their inclusion is recommended for those prepared to utilize them correctly.

Lastly, your first aid kit should be tailored to you and your group's specific needs and the duration and location of your trip. Consider including personal medications, a blister treatment kit for long hikes, and a thermal blanket for cold-weather environments. It's also beneficial to periodically review and update your kit, ensuring medications are within their expiry date and supplies are replenished after use.

Remember, the goal of your first aid kit is to

provide the tools necessary for immediate care and offer peace of mind, allowing you to fully immerse in the bushcraft experience with the confidence that you are prepared to address minor medical needs. As we progress, we'll delve into assessing risks and planning, equipping you with the knowledge to enjoy your wilderness adventures safely.

Assessing Risks and Planning Ahead

In the realm of bushcraft, venturing into the wilderness is not without its risks. While the allure of the great outdoors beckons, it is paramount to approach each adventure with a mindset geared toward safety and preparedness. This section delves into the critical process of assessing risks and planning, ensuring you are well-equipped to handle potential emergencies in the wild.

The first step in risk assessment involves understanding the environment you plan to explore. Different terrains and climates pose unique challenges; for instance, a dense forest may harbor ticks carrying Lyme disease, while arid regions could expose you to heatstroke and dehydration. Researching the specific hazards of your destination is essential. This includes weather patterns, wildlife, and dangers like unstable terrain or toxic plants.

Once you grasp the environmental risks, it's crucial to evaluate your skill level and physical condition. Bushcraft often requires a blend of physical endurance, navigation skills, and survival knowledge. Be honest with yourself about your capabilities and limitations. If you're venturing into a particularly challenging area, consider acquiring new skills or enhancing existing ones through courses or guided practice.

Equally important is the planning phase. This encompasses route planning, informing someone of your itinerary, and estimating the duration of your trip. Always have a contingency plan if you need to alter your route due to unexpected conditions or emergencies. Technology can be a helpful ally here; GPS devices and emergency beacons can provide a safety net but do not rely on them solely. The wilderness can be unpredictable, and electronic devices may fail.

In addition to personal preparation, group dynamics should be noticed if you're not venturing alone. Ensure all members know the plan and establish clear communication and decision-making protocols. Assess the group's overall skill level and ensure that at least one member is proficient in first aid. Collective responsibility and teamwork can significantly enhance safety in bushcraft expeditions.

Lastly, part of planning ahead involves preparing for the unexpected. Despite thorough preparation, emergencies can still occur. Familiarize yourself with basic first aid procedures and carry a well-stocked kit tailored to your adventure's specific risks. Knowing how to respond to common injuries or illnesses in the wilderness can make a critical difference in the outcome of an emergency.

By meticulously assessing risks and planning, you can significantly mitigate the dangers associated with bushcraft and ensure a safer, more enjoyable experience in the wilderness. This proactive approach prepares you for potential challenges. It instills a more profound respect for the natural world and its inherent risks.

Adopting a Mindset for Survival and First Aid

The line between a minor inconvenience and a life-threatening situation can be thin in the wilderness. The ability to adapt, think clearly, and apply first aid knowledge is not just beneficial—it's essential. Adopting a mindset for survival and first aid is about mentally preparing yourself to face and overcome the challenges that nature might throw. This mindset is a blend of resilience, preparedness, and the ability to remain calm under pressure, which is crucial for effective bushcraft first aid.

Resilience is the backbone of survival. The inner strength enables you to bounce back from setbacks and continue moving forward. In bushcraft, resilience might mean enduring discomfort, like cold or hunger, without losing focus on your safety and well-being. It's about maintaining a positive attitude even when things are unplanned. Remember, your mental state can significantly influence your physical condition. A resilient mindset helps conserve energy and keep stress at bay, vital for survival.

On the other hand, preparedness is about having the knowledge and skills before you need them. It involves learning and practicing first aid techniques, understanding how to use the tools at your disposal, and being aware of the potential hazards in your environment. Preparedness means you've equipped yourself mentally and physically for the challenges you might face. This doesn't just include packing the right gear, familiarizing yourself with the area you'll be exploring, and knowing how to respond to the injuries or health issues that could arise.

The most critical aspect of this mindset is the ability to remain calm under pressure. Panic is your greatest enemy in a survival situation. It clouds judgment, wastes energy, and can lead to poor decision-making. Cultivating calmness involves practicing stress management techniques and developing confidence in your skills and knowledge. Breathing exercises, for instance, can effectively manage stress levels and maintain clarity of thought when faced with an emergency.

To adopt this mindset:

1. Start by challenging yourself in controlled environments.
2. Practice your first aid skills regularly, not just in theory but also through practical application.
3. Engage in outdoor activities that push your comfort zone while ensuring you're never in real danger.
4. Reflect on these experiences, identifying what you did well and where you could improve.

This reflective practice builds confidence and reinforces a positive attitude towards overcoming obstacles.

In conclusion, adopting a mindset for survival and

first aid in bushcraft is about more than just knowing what to do; it's about being mentally prepared. It's a combination of resilience, preparedness, and calmness under pressure. By cultivating this mindset, you equip yourself not just to survive but to thrive in the wilderness, ensuring that you can enjoy the beauty and solitude of nature with the confidence that you are prepared for whatever challenges you might face.

1

BASIC FIRST AID SKILLS

Two adventurers performing first aid in the wilderness.

Performing CPR in the Wilderness

Performing CPR (Cardiopulmonary Resuscitation) in the wilderness requires a calm, methodical approach, especially given the potential lack of immediate professional medical assistance. This section outlines the critical steps to take when faced with a situation that necessitates CPR in a remote setting. It's imperative to remember that CPR can be life-saving when someone's breathing or heartbeat has stopped.

First, assess the situation to ensure your safety and the victim's. In the wilderness, hazards include terrain, wildlife, and the victim's condition. Once it's safe to proceed, check the victim for responsiveness by gently shaking their shoulders and asking loudly, "Are you okay?" If there is no response, call for help. If you're alone, you'll have to make a judgment call on whether to leave the victim to seek help or to start CPR immediately.

Next, check the victim's airway to ensure it is clear. Tilt the head back slightly and lift the chin to open the airway. Look, listen, and feel for breathing for no more than 10 seconds. In the absence of breathing, or if the victim is only gasping, begin CPR.

CPR in the wilderness follows the same basic principles as in more urban settings, focusing on chest compressions and rescue breaths. Place the heel of one hand on the center of the victim's chest, with your other hand on top. Interlock your fingers and ensure you're positioned directly above the victim's chest. Using your body weight, compress the chest at least 2 inches deep but not more than 2.4 inches at a rate of 100 to 120 compressions per minute. After every 30 compressions, give two rescue breaths by pinching the victim's nose shut, covering their mouth with yours, and blowing in to make the chest rise.

It's crucial to continue CPR without interruption until signs of life return, professional help arrives, or you are physically unable to continue. Help can be hours away in a wilderness setting, making your efforts vital to the victim's survival.

Remember, the effectiveness of CPR can be influenced by factors unique to the wilderness, such as extreme temperatures, which can affect both the rescuer's and the victim's physical condition. Additionally, modifications might be necessary based on the victim's age, the presence of injuries, or if the rescuer is alone without the possibility of relief.

Performing CPR is physically demanding, especially in a remote environment. If you're alone, periodically reassess the situation to determine if you need help. If you're with a group, rotate the role of rescuer to avoid exhaustion.

This guide is a basic overview, and it's strongly

recommended that anyone who spends time in the wilderness undergo formal training in wilderness first aid and CPR. Such preparation can make the difference between life and death in emergencies far from immediate medical assistance.

Dealing with Bleeding and Wounds

In the wilderness, where medical help may not be immediately accessible, bushcraft enthusiasts must know how to manage bleeding and wounds effectively. This involves practical steps and techniques to control bleeding and clean and dress wounds to prevent infection and promote healing.

When faced with a bleeding wound, the primary goal is to control the bleeding as quickly as possible. This can be achieved by applying direct pressure to the wound with a clean cloth or bandage. If the bleeding is severe and does not stop with direct pressure, a pressure bandage or, in extreme cases, a tourniquet may be necessary. However, using a tourniquet should be considered a last resort due to the risk of tissue damage and should only be applied by someone trained in its use.

Once the bleeding is under control, cleaning the wound to prevent infection is next. Gently rinse away any dirt or debris with clean water. If clean water is unavailable, boiled and cooled water or a mild antiseptic solution can be used. It's important to avoid using alcohol or hydrogen peroxide directly in the wound, as these substances can damage tissue and delay healing.

After cleaning, applying a thin layer of antibiotic ointment, if available, will help prevent infection and keep the wound moist, which aids in healing. The wound should then be covered with a sterile dressing to protect it from further contamination, absorb any ongoing bleeding, and help keep it moist. The dressing should be changed daily or whenever it becomes wet or dirty. The wound should be inspected for signs of infection, such as increased redness, swelling, warmth, or pus, each time the dressing changes.

While minor wounds can often be managed effectively in the field, monitoring the wound closely for signs of infection or other complications is crucial. If the wound does not begin to heal within a few days, or if any signs of infection are noticed, medical attention should be sought as soon as possible. A healthcare professional should also evaluate wounds caused by a deep animal bite, involve a joint, or show signs of severe infection.

In summary, dealing with bleeding and wounds in

the wilderness requires prompt and appropriate action to control bleeding, clean and disinfect the wound, and apply a protective dressing. Following these steps allows most minor wounds to be effectively managed and complications prevented. However, always be prepared to seek medical attention when necessary, as some wounds may require professional care to heal properly.

Managing Sprains and Fractures

In the wilderness, where medical help might be hours or even days away, knowing how to manage sprains and fractures can make a significant difference in mobility and pain management. This section covers practical steps and techniques to effectively address these common injuries, ensuring you can provide the best care in a bushcraft setting.

A sprain occurs when a ligament, the tissue connecting bones, is stretched or torn, typically in the ankles, knees, or wrists. A fracture, on the other hand, is a break in a bone. Both injuries share symptoms like pain, swelling, and limited ability to move the affected area. However, fractures may also present with visible deformity or the sound of a bone breaking at the time of injury.

Upon suspecting a sprain or fracture, the first step is to stop and assess the situation. Encourage the injured person to remain still and support the injured limb in its natural position, avoiding unnecessary movement that could exacerbate the injury.

For sprains, the **RICE** method is a widely recommended treatment plan that includes:

- **Rest** (keeping weight off the injured area)
- **Ice** (applying cold packs to reduce swelling and pain with a barrier like a cloth to prevent ice burn and limiting application to 20 minutes)
- **Compression** (wrapping the injured area with a bandage to limit swelling, ensuring it's snug but not too tight)
- **Elevation** (raising the injured limb above heart level to decrease swelling)

Fractures require immobilization to prevent further injury. If trained and safe, you can create a splint with available materials like sticks or a rolled-up magazine and secure it with bandages or cloth strips. The splint should immobilize the joints above and below the fracture site. However, if unsure about the nature of the injury or how to immobilize it adequately, it's best to leave the limb in the position found and seek professional medical help as soon as possible.

Pain management is crucial, with over-the-counter pain relievers being an option if the injured person can safely ingest them. Keeping the injured person calm and reassured can also help manage pain psychologically.

Regularly monitoring the injured person for signs of shock or worsening symptoms is essential. If the injury is severe or there's no improvement, evacuation to a medical facility becomes necessary. In a bushcraft context, this might mean self-evacuation or activating emergency response systems if available.

In conclusion, managing sprains and fractures in the wilderness requires a calm and methodical approach. By understanding these basic first aid techniques, you can provide essential care to reduce pain and prevent further injury until professional medical help can be reached. Prevention is the best treatment, so always take necessary precautions to avoid injuries when engaging in bushcraft activities.

Recognizing and Treating Hypothermia and Heatstroke

Understanding how to recognize and treat hypothermia and heatstroke is crucial in the wilderness, where the elements can be as much a foe as any other hazard. These conditions represent the body's inability to regulate its temperature, either dropping too low (hypothermia) or rising too high (heatstroke). Both can be life-threatening if not addressed promptly and adequately.

Recognizing and Treating Hypothermia

Hypothermia occurs when the body loses heat faster than it can produce it, causing the core body temperature to fall below 95°F (35°C). It can happen in any environment, not just those covered in snow or ice. Wind, rain, and immersion in cold water can all lead to hypothermia.

Symptoms include shivering (which may cease as hypothermia worsens), confusion, slurred speech, drowsiness, and, in severe cases, loss of consciousness. The person may also exhibit paradoxical undressing, where they begin to remove clothing due to feeling hot when they are cold.

Treatment begins with moving the person to a sheltered environment to protect them from the cold. Remove any wet clothing and replace it with dry, warm layers. Insulate them from the cold ground using sleeping pads or layers of clothing. Warm, sweet beverages can help increase the body's temperature, but avoid alcohol or caffeine. Gentle rewarming is critical; too rapid heating can be dangerous. If available, use warm (not hot) water bottles or heat packs placed in the armpits, groin, and along the sides of the chest. Monitor the person's breathing and be prepared to perform CPR if they become unresponsive.

Recognizing and Treating Heatstroke

Conversely, heatstroke occurs when the body overheats, typically due to prolonged exposure to or physical exertion in high temperatures. The body's temperature regulation system becomes overwhelmed, leading to a core body temperature of 104°F (40°C) or higher.

Symptoms include confusion, altered mental state, slurred speech, nausea, vomiting, rapid breathing, flushed skin, and, in severe cases, loss of consciousness. Unlike heat exhaustion, a precursor to heatstroke, the person may stop sweating.

Treatment focuses on rapidly lowering the body's temperature. Move the person to a shaded or air-conditioned area. Remove excess clothing to increase heat loss. Apply wet cloths to the skin, or immerse the person in cool (not cold) water if possible—fan air over the person while wetting their skin to increase cooling through evaporation. Offer sips of water if the person is conscious and can drink, but do not force fluids. Monitor their condition closely and seek emergency medical help immediately. Heatstroke is a severe condition that requires professional medical treatment.

In both hypothermia and heatstroke, prevention is critical. Dress appropriately for the environment, stay hydrated, and avoid extreme temperature exposures when possible. Understanding these conditions and their treatments empowers you to act decisively, potentially saving lives in the wilderness.

Creating and Using Splints from Natural Materials

In the wilderness, the ability to improvise with available resources can be a lifesaver, especially when it comes to administering first aid. One common scenario where bushcraft skills come into play is in creating and applying splints using natural materials.

This guide will help you identify suitable materials and construct effective splints for different injuries.

The first step in creating a natural splint is finding sturdy yet somewhat flexible materials to support and immobilize the injured limb. Ideal materials include straight, strong branches free of rot or excessive flexibility. They should be longer than the injured area to ensure proper support. Large pieces, like birch bark, are also suitable due to their flexibility and strength. Additionally, flexible vines or roots can keep the splint in place but ensure they are strong enough to hold it without breaking.

Once you have gathered your materials, you should prepare the limb by ensuring the injured area is as comfortable and aligned as possible, avoiding excessive movement, especially if a fracture is suspected. If possible, pad the injured area with soft materials such as moss, leaves, or clothing to prevent pressure sores and discomfort. Then, place the rigid materials (sticks, branches, or bark) along the injured limb's sides, ensuring they extend beyond the joints above and below the injury. A single splint along the injured digit may suffice for fingers or toes.

Securing the splint involves using vines, roots, strips of fabric, or even shoelaces to tie the splint in place. Start by securing the splint above and below the injury site, avoiding tying directly over the injury. The ties should be firm to immobilize the limb but not so tight as to cut off circulation. You can check for adequate blood flow by pressing on a fingernail or toenail; the color should return within a few seconds.

After applying the splint, monitoring the injured person for signs of decreased circulation, such as increased pain, swelling, or a bluish tint to the skin, is essential. Adjust the splint as necessary to ensure comfort and safety. While creating and applying a splint from natural materials can be crucial in a wilderness emergency, it is temporary. Always seek professional medical help as soon as possible. Suppose you need clarification about the severity of the injury or how to apply a splint properly. In that case, it's better to immobilize the limb with soft padding and seek help rather than risk further injury by misapplying a splint.

In conclusion, creating and using splints from natural materials is a valuable skill in bushcraft first aid. By following these guidelines, you can provide essential support to an injured limb and prevent further damage while awaiting professional medical care. Remember, the key to adequate first aid is a calm and methodical approach, ensuring the safety and comfort of the injured person throughout the process.

Chapter Summary

- Performing CPR in the wilderness requires a calm approach and immediate action, focusing on chest compressions and rescue breaths.
- Ensure personal and victim safety before proceeding with CPR, checking for responsiveness and breathing before starting compressions.
- Continue CPR without interruption until professional help arrives or the victim shows signs of life.
- Wilderness conditions, such as extreme temperatures, may affect CPR effectiveness and require modifications based on the victim's condition.
- Managing bleeding involves applying direct pressure, cleaning and disinfecting the wound, and using a sterile dressing to promote healing.
- Sprains and fractures should be managed using the RICE method for sprains and immobilization for fractures, with pain

management and monitoring for complications.
- Recognizing and treating hypothermia and heatstroke are crucial in wilderness settings, focusing on rewarming or cooling the victim, respectively.
- Creating splints from natural materials involves finding sturdy supports, securing them to immobilize the injured limb, and monitoring circulation issues.

2
NATURAL REMEDIES AND PLANT MEDICINE

An array of medicinal plants and herbs on a workbench.

Identifying Medicinal Plants

In the wilderness, identifying medicinal plants is crucial for emergency first aid and long-term survival skills.

This knowledge allows for the treatment of various ailments with natural remedies. It fosters a deep connection with the natural environment. The process involves recognizing and utilizing medicinal plants, focusing on their identification, harvesting, and the ethical considerations involved.

The initial step in using plant medicine is to identify the plants accurately. This requires observation skills and sometimes a bit of study. Start by familiarizing yourself with a few common plants in your area, learning about their characteristics, habitats, and any similar-looking plants that could be harmful. Using field guides specific to your region, which provide detailed descriptions and photographs, can be extremely helpful.

Additionally, joining a local foraging group or workshop can offer hands-on experience with the guidance of experts.

When identifying plants, it's essential to examine their leaves, flowers, stems, and roots closely, noting their shape, color, and distinctive features. Some plants may only be identifiable when they bloom, while others can be recognized by their foliage or bark. Understanding botanical terminology can significantly improve your identification skills, making understanding and sharing your findings more accessible.

After positively identifying a plant as medicinal and safe, the next step is to harvest it responsibly. This means taking only what you need and ensuring the plant can continue to thrive. Use clean, sharp tools for precise cuts, aiding the plant's recovery. The timing of harvesting is also vital to preserving the plant's medicinal properties; for example, leaves and flowers are best collected in the morning when their essential oils are most concentrated. At the same time, roots are typically harvested in the fall.

Ethical foraging is essential when collecting medicinal plants. This includes getting permission to forage on private land, respecting protected areas, and avoiding endangered species. Sustainable foraging practices are crucial, such as taking only what you need and leaving no trace. It's also important to consider the ecological impact of removing plants from their habitat and harvesting in a way that allows plant populations to regenerate.

In summary, identifying and harvesting medicinal plants are critical skills in bushcraft first aid, offering a way to harness nature's healing power. By practicing these skills with respect, care, and a willingness to learn, you can use plant medicine safely and sustainably to support health and well-being in the wilderness. The following steps involve transforming these raw materials into effective poultices and salves, further enhancing your bushcraft first aid capabilities.

Preparing Poultices and Salves

In bushcraft first aid, preparing poultices and salves from natural resources can be a vital skill for treating various injuries and ailments when conventional medical supplies are unavailable. This section delves into the practical aspects of creating these remedies using medicinal plants identified in the wild.

A poultice is a soft, moist mass of plant material applied directly to the skin to relieve soreness and inflammation. It can treat insect bites, stings, cuts, bruises, and infections. To prepare a poultice, follow these steps:

1. **Select the appropriate plant:** Based on the ailment, choose a plant known for its medicinal properties. For example, plantain leaves (Plantago major) are excellent for cuts and insect bites due to their anti-inflammatory and antiseptic properties.

2. **Crush or grind the plant material:** Use a mortar and pestle, a stone, or simply your hands to crush the leaves, roots, or flowers of the plant to release its medicinal compounds. Adding a small amount of water can help if the plant is too dry.
3. **Apply to the affected area:** Spread the crushed plant material directly onto the skin over the affected area. If the injury is open, ensure the plant material is clean and free from contaminants.
4. **Secure the poultice:** Use a clean cloth or bandage to hold the poultice in place. It's essential to keep the poultice moist for its active components to be effective.
5. **Duration:** Leave the poultice on for up to 4 hours. Monitor the skin for adverse reactions, such as increased irritation or allergies.

Salves, or ointments, are thickened preparations to heal and protect the skin. They are handy for treating dry skin, chapped lips, burns, and wounds. To make an essential herbal salve:

1. **Infuse oils with medicinal plants:** Begin by infusing a carrier oil (such as coconut oil, olive oil, or almond oil) with your chosen medicinal plant. This can be done by gently heating the oil and plant material in a double boiler for 2-3 hours, ensuring the oil does not overheat.
2. **Strain the plant material:** After the infusion process, strain the oil through a fine mesh strainer or cheesecloth to remove the plant material, leaving behind the infused oil.
3. **Thicken the salve:** Add beeswax to the infused oil. A general guideline is to use approximately 1 ounce (28 grams) of beeswax per cup (240 ml) of infused oil. Gently heat the mixture until the beeswax melts completely.
4. **Cool and solidify:** Pour the mixture into clean containers and allow it to cool and solidify. Adding essential oils for additional therapeutic benefits can be done at this stage, ensuring they are thoroughly mixed before the salve hardens.

5. **Storage:** Store the salve in a cool, dark place. Properly made salves can last for up to a year.

By mastering the preparation of poultices and salves, one can effectively utilize the healing power of nature. These traditional remedies, derived from the knowledge of identifying medicinal plants, offer a sustainable and accessible form of first aid in the wilderness. As we progress, understanding the role of natural antiseptics will further enhance our ability to manage injuries and infections in a bushcraft setting.

Natural Antiseptics in the Wild

Nature offers its pharmacy in the wilderness, where conventional medical supplies might not be readily available. Understanding how to harness the natural antiseptics found in the wild can be a crucial skill for anyone practicing bushcraft or simply spending time in nature. This section delves into identifying and using natural antiseptics to prevent infection and promote healing in cuts, scrapes, and other wounds.

One of the most readily available natural antiseptics is honey. Known for its antibacterial properties, honey can be applied directly to wounds to prevent infection and promote healing. Its high viscosity helps to create a protective barrier over the wound, keeping it clean and moist, which is conducive to healing. When sourcing honey in the wild, ensure it is from a clean and uncontaminated source.

Another powerful natural antiseptic is garlic. Garlic contains allicin, a compound with significant antibacterial and antifungal properties. Crushing fresh garlic cloves and applying them to wounds can help prevent infection. However, due to its potency, it's advisable to use garlic cautiously as it can cause skin irritation in some individuals.

The sap of certain trees, such as pine or birch, also serves as an effective natural antiseptic. These saps contain compounds that inhibit the growth of bacteria and fungi. To use, apply a small amount of sap directly to the wound. The sap not only helps prevent infection but can also act as a natural bandage, sealing the wound from external contaminants.

Aloe vera is another valuable natural antiseptic widely recognized for its soothing and healing properties. The gel inside the aloe vera leaves can be applied to wounds to reduce inflammation and fight bacteria. Its cooling effect relieves pain and itching associated with minor wounds and burns.

Lastly, the plantain leaf, commonly found in many parts of the world, is an effective wound remedy. The leaves contain antibacterial and anti-inflammatory properties. Crushed or chewed plantain leaves can be applied directly to the wound or as a poultice. This not only helps prevent infection but also soothes the affected area.

Incorporating these natural antiseptics into your bushcraft first aid kit can significantly enhance your ability to manage wounds effectively in the wild. It's important to remember that while these natural remedies can be beneficial, they are not substitutes for professional medical treatment in serious cases. Always seek medical attention for severe wounds or if there's a risk of infection that doesn't improve with basic first aid measures.

Using Herbs for Pain Relief

Understanding the natural resources available for managing pain is vital in bushcraft and wilderness survival. This section delves into the practical use of herbs for pain relief, a cornerstone of natural remedies and plant medicine. It's important to note that while these methods can provide relief, they should not replace professional medical treatment when it's available. However, these natural solutions can be invaluable in situations where conventional medicine is not an option.

Willow bark, often referred to as nature's aspirin, contains salicin, a chemical similar to the active ingredient in aspirin. Various cultures have harnessed willow bark's properties for centuries to alleviate pain and reduce fever. To use willow bark for pain relief, one can chew on the bark directly or brew a tea. To prepare the tea, simmer about two teaspoons of shredded bark in a cup of water for 10 to 15 minutes, then let it steep for an additional half hour. Drinking this tea can help ease pain from headaches, lower back discomfort, and arthritis. Use of willow bark judiciously is crucial, as excessive consumption can lead to stomach irritation or more severe health issues.

Turmeric is a powerful anti-inflammatory herb that can treat many pains and aches, especially inflammation-related. The active component in turmeric, curcumin, is responsible for its pain-relieving effects. Incorporating turmeric into your diet or applying a paste made from turmeric powder and water to the affected area can help reduce inflammation and alleviate pain. For internal use, adding a teaspoon of turmeric to a warm drink or meal daily can offer systemic pain relief.

Lavender is renowned for its calming and soothing

properties, making it an excellent herb for relieving stress and tension headaches. The aroma of lavender alone can act as a mild sedative, helping to reduce pain perception. For topical application, lavender oil can be diluted with carrier oil and massaged into the temples or the back of the neck to alleviate headache pain. Additionally, inhaling lavender essential oil or using it in a diffuser can help create a relaxing environment conducive to pain relief.

Peppermint is another herb with significant pain-relieving properties, particularly for digestive discomfort and headaches. The menthol in peppermint acts as a natural analgesic, providing a cooling sensation that can soothe pain. For headaches, applying diluted peppermint oil to the forehead has been shown to reduce the intensity and duration of pain. Peppermint tea is an effective remedy to alleviate digestive issues. Steep a teaspoon of dried peppermint leaves in boiling water for 10 minutes, strain, and drink.

Ginger, with its potent anti-inflammatory and analgesic properties, is effective in treating a variety of pains, including menstrual cramps and joint pain. Ginger can be consumed fresh, dried, as a tea, or applied topically. For pain relief, drinking ginger tea is particularly beneficial. To make ginger tea, simmer a piece of fresh ginger root in water for 15 to 20 minutes, then strain and enjoy. Ginger's warmth not only alleviates pain but also helps improve circulation, which can speed up the healing process.

Incorporating these herbs into your bushcraft first aid kit can provide natural, effective options for managing pain in the wilderness. Remember, the key to using any natural remedy is knowledge and moderation. Understanding the correct preparation and dosage is crucial to ensuring these remedies are safe and effective. As we transition from discussing natural pain relief methods, it's essential to consider the broader context of health and healing in the wilderness, including the role of nutrition in supporting the body's recovery processes.

The Role of Nutrition in Healing

In the wilderness, where conventional medical resources are scarce, the importance of nutrition in healing cannot be overstated. The body's ability to repair itself, fight infections, and recover from injuries is significantly enhanced by the nutrients we consume. This section delves into the role of nutrition in healing, focusing on how certain foods and natural resources found in the wild can bolster our health and aid in recovery.

First and foremost, it's essential to understand that a balanced diet is critical in maintaining overall health and optimizing the body's healing processes. Essential nutrients such as proteins, vitamins, minerals, and antioxidants contribute to tissue repair, immune function, and the reduction of inflammation.

Proteins are the building blocks of the body, essential for the repair of tissues and creating new cells. In a bushcraft scenario, protein sources might include fish, wild game, insects, and certain plants and nuts. Consuming adequate amounts of protein can significantly speed up the healing process of wounds and injuries.

Vitamins and minerals, particularly vitamins A, C, D, and E, along with zinc, iron, and selenium, play pivotal roles in healing and immune function. Vitamin C, found in wild berries and certain greens, produces collagen. This protein helps heal wounds by repairing damaged skin and tissues. Vitamin A, sourced from leafy green vegetables and some animal products, supports cell growth and boosts the immune system. Meanwhile, vitamin D, obtained from sunlight exposure, aids in calcium absorption and bone healing.

Antioxidants in various wild plants and fruits combat oxidative stress and reduce inflammation, which is vital in the healing process. Foods rich in antioxidants include berries, nuts, and herbs that can be foraged in the wild.

Hydration is another critical aspect of nutrition in healing. Water is essential for all bodily functions, including transporting nutrients to cells and removing toxins from the body. Ensuring adequate hydration is a simple yet effective way to support the body's natural healing processes.

Incorporating wild edibles into your diet can provide these essential nutrients when conventional food sources are unavailable. Foraging for wild plants, however, requires knowledge of safe and nutritious options specific to the area. Some common edible plants include dandelions, which are rich in vitamins A and C, and nettles, a good source of protein, vitamins, and minerals.

Understanding the nutritional value of available resources and how they can support the body's healing processes is a valuable skill in bushcraft first aid. By prioritizing nutrition and making informed choices about the foods we consume in the wilderness, we can enhance our resilience, accelerate healing, and maintain optimal health in challenging environments.

Chapter Summary

- Medicinal plants are essential for emergency first aid and survival in the wilderness, offering natural treatment options and a deeper environmental connection.
- Identifying medicinal plants accurately requires knowledge of their features, habitats, and similar species, with field guides and local groups as critical resources.
- Harvest medicinal plants respectfully and sustainably, using clean tools and ensuring plants can regrow. Depending on the plant part needed, specific harvesting times are required.
- Ethical foraging involves getting permission, respecting protected areas, avoiding endangered species, and practicing sustainability to allow plant regeneration.
- Preparing poultices and salves includes selecting the appropriate plant, crushing or grinding it, applying it directly, or infusing it in oils with beeswax for salves.
- In a natural first aid kit, natural antiseptics like honey, garlic, tree sap, aloe vera, and

plantain leaf are crucial for preventing infection and aiding wound healing.
- Herbs such as willow bark, turmeric, lavender, peppermint, and ginger offer natural pain relief through teas, pastes, and infused oils.
- Nutrition, including proteins, vitamins, minerals, antioxidants, and hydration, is vital for healing, immune function, and health. It emphasizes the importance of a balanced diet and foraging for wild edibles.

3

HANDLING ANIMAL AND INSECT BITES

A first aid kit in the wilderness.

Identifying Dangerous Animals and Insects

In the wilderness, identifying potentially dangerous animals and insects is crucial for ensuring your safety and well-being. This knowledge helps avoid unwanted encounters and prepares you for the appropriate response in case of a bite or sting. The variety of fauna that one might encounter is vast. Still, specific characteristics and behaviors can help in recognizing the threats.

Starting with snakes, many species are harmless, but it's the venomous ones that bushcraft enthusiasts need to be wary of. Venomous snakes can often be identified by their distinctive head shapes, which are usually broader and more triangular than non-venomous snakes due to their venom glands. Additionally, in some regions, elliptical pupils can indicate venomous species. However, these characteristics are not universal, and learning about the specific snake species in your activity area is highly recommended.

Spiders are another group of concern. While the vast majority are harmless, there are a few species, such as the Black Widow and the Brown Recluse, whose bites can cause serious health issues. These spiders tend to be reclusive and only bite when threatened. Recognizing their distinctive markings and preferred habitats can prevent unwanted encounters. For instance, the Black Widow is known for its shiny black color and the red hourglass shape on its underside.

Insects, including bees, wasps, and hornets, can also

pose risks, especially to individuals with allergies to their stings. These insects are generally more aggressive when their nests are disturbed. Recognizing nest sites and understanding these insects' behavior can help avoid them. For example, wasps and hornets can be more aggressive and are likely to attack in swarms if their nests, often found hanging from trees or under eaves, are disturbed.

Ticks, though small, are significant carriers of diseases such as Lyme disease. They are often found in wooded or grassy areas and can attach to the skin of humans and animals. Checking for ticks and knowing how to remove them safely is crucial after spending time in their habitats.

Understanding these animals' and insects' behavior and habitat is critical to avoiding dangerous encounters. For instance, many venomous snakes are more active at night, and avoiding their habitats during these times can reduce the risk of encounters. Similarly, wearing protective clothing and being vigilant in areas known to harbor ticks can prevent bites.

In conclusion, the ability to identify potentially dangerous animals and insects is an essential component of bushcraft first aid. It enables individuals to take preventive measures and apply the correct first aid procedures in case of an encounter. Knowledge of the local fauna and an understanding of their behavior and habitats is invaluable for anyone venturing into the wilderness.

First Aid for Snake Bites

In the wilderness, encountering a snake and, worse, suffering a bite can be a harrowing experience. However, the situation can be managed effectively with the proper knowledge and actions. This section delves into the first aid measures that should be taken if someone is bitten by a snake, focusing on practical and immediate steps to mitigate the effects of the bite and ensure the victim's safety until professional medical help can be reached.

First and foremost, it's crucial to remain calm. Panic can accelerate the heart rate, potentially causing the venom to spread more quickly through the body. Keep the victim as still as possible, reassuring them that help is coming. Identifying the snake can be helpful for treatment, but it should not jeopardize anyone's safety. If possible, take note of the snake's appearance from a safe distance.

The next step is immobilizing the bitten limb, but avoid applying a tourniquet or cutting into the wound. These outdated methods can cause more harm than good. Instead, gently wash the bite area with soap and water, if available, to remove any venom on the skin surface. Cover the bite with a clean, dry dressing to protect it from infection.

It's imperative to keep the bitten limb immobilized and as still as possible, ideally at or slightly below heart level. This helps to slow the spread of venom. Construct a splint, if necessary, using whatever materials are at hand to prevent movement of the affected area.

Do not administer any medications, including painkillers or anti-inflammatory drugs, unless advised by a medical professional. Also, refrain from giving the victim anything to eat or drink, especially alcohol or caffeine, as these substances could exacerbate the body's reaction to the venom.

Seeking medical assistance immediately is the most critical step. If in a remote location, send someone for help or use a communication device to call emergency services. Provide them with as much information as possible about the situation, including the type of snake, if known, the time of the bite, and the victim's current condition.

While waiting for help to arrive, monitor the victim closely for any signs of shock or changes in their condition. Keep them warm, comfortable, and still.

Reassure them that help is on the way and that staying calm is essential for their recovery.

In summary, the key to handling snake bites effectively is to remain calm, immobilize and protect the bite area, avoid harmful interventions, and seek professional medical help immediately. By following these steps, you can provide essential first aid that could make a significant difference in the outcome for the victim.

Treating Insect Stings and Bites

In the wilderness, insect stings and bites are not only shared. Still, they can also pose significant risks if not treated properly. This section provides a comprehensive guide to managing these incidents, ensuring safety and minimizing discomfort.

When dealing with insect stings, the first step is to remain calm. Panic can accelerate the spread of venom in the body. It should be removed if the stinger is still present, as is often the case with bee stings. However, care must be taken to scrape it out sideways with a fingernail or a blunt object like a credit card rather than tweezers, which can squeeze more venom into the skin.

Once the stinger is removed, wash the area with soap and water to prevent infection. Applying cold compresses or ice packs can help reduce swelling and pain. It's crucial to monitor for signs of an allergic reaction, including difficulty breathing, swelling of the face or mouth, or a rash spreading away from the bite site. In such cases, immediate medical attention is necessary.

For bites from insects such as mosquitoes, flies, and ants, the emphasis should be on alleviating itching and discomfort while preventing infection. After washing the affected area, applying a soothing lotion or cream containing hydrocortisone or calamine can provide relief. An oral antihistamine may also help reduce itching and swelling. To avoid infection, refrain from scratching the bite. If signs of infection such as increased redness, swelling, or pus develop, seek medical attention.

In cases of multiple stings or bites, or if the victim is known to have severe allergic reactions, it's imperative to seek medical help immediately. Carrying an epinephrine auto-injector (EpiPen) and antihistamines can be life-saving for individuals with known severe allergies.

Preventive measures are also a key component of managing insect stings and bites. Wearing protective clothing, using insect repellent, and avoiding scented products can significantly reduce the risk of being bitten or stung. Additionally, being aware of one's surroundings and avoiding areas known for high insect activity, such as stagnant water or dense woods, can minimize encounters with potentially harmful insects.

Following these guidelines, individuals can effectively manage insect stings and bites, ensuring a safer and more enjoyable wilderness experience.

Preventing and Treating Tick Bites

In the wilderness, ticks are not merely a nuisance; they are carriers of Lyme disease, Rocky Mountain spotted fever, and several other tick-borne illnesses. Understanding how to prevent tick bites and properly remove a tick is crucial for anyone venturing into tick-prone areas.

Preventing tick bites begins with the proper clothing and gear. Wear long sleeves and long pants when moving through areas known for ticks, such as wooded or grassy areas. Tuck your pants into your socks to create a barrier against ticks climbing up your legs. Light-colored clothing can make it easier to spot ticks before they find their way to your skin.

Applying insect repellent that contains 20% or more DEET, picaridin, or IR3535 on exposed skin and clothing can significantly reduce the risk of tick bites.

Treat clothing and gear, such as boots, pants, and tents, with products containing 0.5% permethrin for added protection. It's essential to follow the product instructions for proper application and reapplication.

After spending time in tick-infested areas, conduct a thorough tick check on yourself, your children, and your pets. Pay close attention to under the arms, in and around the ears, inside the belly button, behind the knees, between the legs, around the waist, and especially in the hair. Showering within two hours of coming indoors can help wash off unattached ticks and provide an excellent opportunity to conduct a tick check.

If you find a tick attached to your skin, removing it as soon as possible is essential. The longer a tick is attached, the greater the risk of disease transmission. Use fine-tipped tweezers to grasp the tick as close to the skin's surface as possible. Pull upward with steady, even pressure. Do not twist or jerk the tick, which can cause the mouth parts to break off and remain in the skin. If this happens, attempt to remove the mouth parts with the tweezers. If unable to remove the mouth entirely, leave it alone and let the skin heal.

After removing the tick, thoroughly clean the bite area and your hands with rubbing alcohol, an iodine scrub, or soap and water. Dispose of a live tick by submerging it in alcohol, placing it in a sealed bag/container, wrapping it tightly in tape, or flushing it down the toilet. Never crush a tick with your fingers.

Monitor the bite site for several weeks for signs of tick-borne illness, such as rash or fever. If you develop symptoms, consult a healthcare provider promptly. Be sure to tell them about the recent tick bite, when it occurred, and where you most likely acquired it.

Understanding and implementing these preventive measures and tick removal techniques can significantly reduce the risks associated with tick bites. The following section will delve into the prevention and first response to another critical concern in the wilderness: rabies.

Rabies Prevention and First Response

The risk of encountering animals that may carry rabies is a genuine concern for bushcraft enthusiasts in the wilderness. Rabies is a fatal viral disease affecting mammals' central nervous system, including humans. It is transmitted through the saliva of infected animals, typically through bites. This section provides a comprehensive guide on rabies prevention and the first response to potential rabies exposure in a bushcraft setting.

Preventing rabies starts with understanding and avoiding unnecessary risks. Here are essential preventive measures:

1. **Vaccination:** If you're planning extended stays in areas known for rabies, consider getting vaccinated before your trip. Rabies pre-exposure vaccination involves a series of injections that provide protection but do not eliminate the need for additional treatment if bitten.
2. **Wildlife Awareness:** Educate yourself about the wildlife in the area you'll be exploring. Avoid attracting or approaching wild animals, especially if they appear sick or behave unusually.
3. **Secure Food and Trash:** Animals, including potential rabies carriers like raccoons, bats, and foxes, are attracted to food. Store your food securely and manage your trash to avoid attracting them to your campsite.
4. **Pet Protection:** If your bushcraft adventure includes pets, ensure they are vaccinated against rabies. Keep pets on a leash and under close supervision.

Swift action is crucial if an animal bites you or someone in your group. Here's what to do:

1. **Immediate Care:** Wash the wound thoroughly with soap and water for at least 15 minutes. This can significantly reduce the viral load.
2. **Stop the Bleeding:** Apply gentle pressure with a clean cloth to stop bleeding.
3. **Disinfect:** After washing, apply an antiseptic solution to the wound to minimize infection risk.
4. **Seek Medical Attention:** Even if the wound seems minor, seeking a professional medical evaluation as soon as possible is essential. Inform the healthcare provider about the bite and your concerns about rabies.
5. **Observe the Animal:** If it's safe, observe the animal from a distance. Information about its behavior and appearance can be crucial for healthcare providers. However, do not attempt to capture or kill the animal yourself.
6. **Follow-Up:** Post-exposure prophylaxis (PEP) injections may be necessary if rabies

exposure is suspected. The treatment is highly effective if started promptly.

Remember, while the wilderness offers remarkable experiences, it poses unique challenges. Rabies prevention and how to respond to animal bites are critical components of bushcraft first aid. By taking preventive measures and being prepared to act quickly in case of an animal bite, you can enjoy your bushcraft adventures with greater peace of mind.

Chapter Summary

- Recognize dangerous animals and insects (e.g., venomous snakes, Black Widow, Brown Recluse) for safety.
- Understand the aggressive behaviors of bees, wasps, hornets, and disease risks from ticks.
- Treat snake bites by remaining calm, immobilizing the limb, washing the area, and seeking immediate medical help.
- Handle insect stings by removing the stinger carefully, washing the area, applying cold compresses, and watching for allergies.

- Prevent tick bites with protective clothing, insect repellent, thorough checks, and prompt tick removal.
- Avoid rabies by getting vaccinated, avoiding wild animals, securing food/trash, and ensuring pet vaccinations.
- Immediate, correct response to bites or stings includes washing, disinfecting, immobilizing the area, and getting medical advice.
- Knowledge of local wildlife, behaviors, habitats, and preventive measures, such as appropriate clothing and repellents, is crucial for wilderness safety.

4

WATER SAFETY AND HYDRATION

An adventurer purifying water in the wilderness.

Finding and Purifying Water

Finding and purifying water is a critical skill for survival in the wilderness. Still, recognizing when your body needs hydration is equally important. Dehydration can occur more quickly than many realize, especially in hot, dry, or high-altitude environments. Understanding the signs of dehydration is essential for anyone venturing into the outdoors, as it can prevent serious health issues and ensure a safe return from your adventures.

The initial signs of dehydration are often subtle and easily overlooked, especially during activities that demand your focus. Thirst is the most obvious indicator, yet you're already dehydrated by the time you feel thirsty. This is why drinking water at regular intervals, especially during physical exertion, is crucial rather than waiting to feel thirsty.

Other early signs include dry mouth, fatigue, and decreased urine output. Urine color is a valuable indicator of hydration levels; light, straw-colored urine typically signifies adequate hydration, whereas dark yellow or amber-colored urine is a clear sign of dehydration. Monitoring these signs closely is essential, as they can quickly escalate to more severe symptoms if not addressed.

As dehydration progresses, symptoms become more pronounced, including headache, dizziness, or lightheadedness, particularly when standing up. These symptoms are often accompanied by dry skin, decreased sweat production, and muscle cramps. In severe cases, dehydration can lead to confusion, rapid heartbeat, rapid breathing, and even fainting. If any of these severe symptoms occur, seeking medical attention immediately is imperative.

To prevent dehydration, start by ensuring you're well-hydrated before embarking on any outdoor activities. Carry sufficient water supplies and plan for ways to replenish your water if you will be out for extended periods. Remember, in hot or humid conditions or at high altitudes, your body will require more water than usual. Additionally, incorporating electrolyte-replenishing drinks or snacks can help maintain the balance of fluids and electrolytes in your body, especially during prolonged exertion.

In summary, recognizing the signs of dehydration is a fundamental aspect of bushcraft first aid. By staying vigilant and proactive about hydration, you can prevent dehydration and its potentially dangerous consequences, ensuring a safer and more enjoyable wilderness experience.

Recognizing Signs of Dehydration

In the wilderness, where resources can be scarce, and conditions are harsh, maintaining proper hydration is not just a matter of comfort but of survival. Dehydration can set in quickly, especially during the strenuous activities often associated with bushcraft, such as hiking, building shelters, or even finding and purifying water itself. Recognizing the signs of dehydration early is crucial to prevent a manageable situation from escalating into a life-threatening emergency.

Dehydration occurs when your body loses more fluids than it takes in, leading to an imbalance that affects its normal functions. The initial symptoms can be subtle and easily overlooked, especially when your focus is on the tasks at hand. Surprisingly, thirst is not the most reliable indicator, as you may already be dehydrated by the time you feel thirsty. Instead, look for other early signs, such as a dry or sticky mouth, fatigue, and decreased urine output. The color of your urine is a valuable indicator of your hydration status; a pale straw color suggests adequate hydration, while darker shades indicate dehydration.

As dehydration progresses, the symptoms become more pronounced and harder to ignore. You may experience dizziness, confusion, or irritability, impairing your judgment and physical performance. Severe dehydration can lead to more alarming signs, including a rapid but weak pulse, low blood pressure, and sunken eyes. In extreme cases, delirium or unconsciousness can occur, signaling a medical emergency that requires immediate attention.

It's important to understand that dehydration can exacerbate the effects of other illnesses and conditions, making it harder for the body to cope with infections or recover from injuries. Furthermore, preventing dehydration becomes even more critical in a bushcraft setting, where medical help may not be readily available.

To combat dehydration, start by ensuring you consume adequate water regularly, even if you do not feel thirsty. Pay attention to the color of your urine as a gauge for your hydration levels, and adjust your fluid intake accordingly. In environments where sweating is likely, such as during physical exertion or in hot climates, increase your water intake to compensate for the loss of fluids through sweat. Additionally, be mindful of the signs of dehydration in yourself and others, especially in a group. Early detection and prompt action can prevent dehydration from becoming a severe threat to your health and safety in the wilderness.

In conclusion, recognizing the signs of dehydration is a fundamental skill in bushcraft first aid. By staying informed and vigilant, you can ensure that you and your

Treating Waterborne Illnesses

In the wilderness, water is both a life-sustaining resource and a potential source of illness. When hydration becomes a matter of concern, it's crucial to understand how to find and purify water and treat waterborne illnesses that might arise despite precautions. This section delves into the practical steps and knowledge required to manage such conditions, ensuring your bushcraft adventures remain safe and enjoyable.

In untreated water sources, waterborne illnesses are primarily caused by pathogens such as bacteria, viruses, and protozoa. Symptoms can range from mild gastrointestinal discomfort to severe dehydration and, in extreme cases, life-threatening conditions. Recognizing the signs of these illnesses early on is critical to effective treatment and recovery.

The first step in treating waterborne illnesses is to ensure the affected individual remains hydrated. Dehydration can exacerbate symptoms and lead to more severe health issues. Begin by providing small, frequent sips of clean, purified water. Avoid giving large amounts of water at once, as this can overwhelm the digestive system of someone already ill.

Oral rehydration solutions (ORS) are particularly effective in preventing dehydration caused by diarrhea and vomiting, common symptoms of waterborne diseases. These solutions, which can be pre-packaged or made by mixing six teaspoons of sugar and half a teaspoon of salt in 1 liter of purified water, help replenish lost fluids and electrolytes. It's advisable to have ORS packets as part of your first aid kit when venturing into the wilderness.

In cases where symptoms persist or worsen, seeking medical attention is crucial. Some waterborne illnesses may require antibiotics or specific treatments that can only be prescribed by a healthcare professional; however, in remote areas where immediate medical help is unavailable, knowing how to recognize and manage the initial symptoms can be life-saving.

Preventive measures are equally important to prevent waterborne illnesses. Always purify water by boiling, filtering, or using chemical treatments before drinking or using it for cooking. Be mindful of your water sources, avoiding those likely to be contaminated by human or animal waste.

Understanding the risks and symptoms of

waterborne illnesses and knowing how to treat and prevent them is essential for anyone venturing into the wilderness. You can enjoy the natural world with confidence and security by ensuring access to clean, safe water and being prepared to address any health issues that arise.

Safe Swimming Practices

Water is both a vital resource and a potential hazard in the wilderness. While we've discussed the importance of treating water to prevent illness, addressing the risks associated with swimming in natural water bodies is equally crucial. Safe swimming practices in the wilderness are about personal safety, preserving one's health, and ensuring that water sources remain uncontaminated and safe for consumption.

First and foremost, always assess the water conditions before deciding to swim. Look for signs of pollution or contamination, such as floating debris, oil slicks, or unusual colors and odors. Remember, water safe for swimming is only necessarily safe for drinking if adequately treated.

Be mindful of the water's current and depth. Even the most experienced swimmers can be caught off guard by sudden changes in depth or unexpected undercurrents. Avoid swimming in fast-moving rivers or streams, as these can quickly become dangerous. If you're unfamiliar with the area, ask locals or refer to guides about safe swimming spots.

It's also important to never swim alone. Having a buddy ensures that help is readily available in an emergency. Additionally, always inform someone on the shore of your swimming plans, including your expected return time.

Before entering the water, take a moment to acclimate to the temperature. Sudden immersion in cold water can lead to shock and hypothermia, impairing your ability to swim and make rational decisions. Gradually enter the water to allow your body to adjust.

Be cautious of wildlife. Many water bodies in the wilderness are home to snakes, leeches, and other potentially dangerous animals. Research the local wildlife and understand the risks before deciding to swim. Avoid areas known for harboring dangerous species.

Lastly, consider the impact of your swimming on the environment. If you plan to bathe, use biodegradable soap and avoid introducing foreign substances into the water. Remember, preserving the natural purity of wilderness water sources is essential for the health of the ecosystem and the safety of all who rely on it.

By adhering to these safe swimming practices, you can enjoy the refreshing and invigorating experience of swimming in the wild while minimizing risks to yourself and the environment. As we transition from understanding the risks associated with water to exploring strategies for staying hydrated in the wilderness, it's clear that water plays a multifaceted role in bushcraft and survival. Proper respect and understanding of this vital resource are critical to a safe and enjoyable wilderness experience.

Chapter Summary

- Finding and purifying water is crucial in the wilderness, as is recognizing signs of dehydration to prevent health issues.
- Initial signs of dehydration include thirst, dry mouth, fatigue, and decreased urine output. Urine color is a crucial indicator of hydration levels.
- Severe dehydration symptoms include headache, dizziness, dry skin, muscle cramps, confusion, rapid heartbeat, and

fainting, necessitating immediate medical attention.
- Preventing dehydration involves starting well-hydrated, carrying sufficient water, and replenishing electrolytes, especially in hot, humid, or high-altitude conditions.
- Recognizing early signs of dehydration, such as a dry mouth and dark urine, is crucial in bushcraft and survival to prevent life-threatening emergencies.
- Treating waterborne illnesses involves staying hydrated, using oral rehydration solutions, and seeking medical attention for severe or persistent symptoms.
- Safe swimming practices in the wilderness include assessing water conditions, being cautious of wildlife, and minimizing environmental impact.

5

FOOD SAFETY AND NUTRITION

Two campers preparing food at a campsite.

Foraging for Edible Plants

Foraging for edible plants is a fundamental skill in bushcraft and survival, significantly enhancing food safety and nutrition. This skill involves identifying, harvesting, and preparing wild plants to supplement one's diet in the wilderness. It's essential to forage with respect for nature and understand the potential risks.

The first step in foraging is learning to identify edible plants accurately. Misidentification can lead to consuming toxic species, resulting in illness or worse. It's essential to familiarize yourself with the area's flora you'll be exploring by studying guidebooks, attending workshops, or participating in guided walks led by experienced foragers or botanists.

Start by focusing on a few easily recognizable and widely available plants, such as dandelions, which can be eaten entirely; nettles, which are excellent when cooked to remove their sting; and wild garlic, identifiable by its distinctive smell. The key to safe foraging is certainty; if you're not 100% sure of a plant's identity, do not eat it.

Sustainable harvesting practices are crucial to ensure that plant populations remain healthy and abundant for future foragers. It's advisable to take at most a third of what's available in a given area to preserve the ecosystem and allow plants to grow and propagate. Be mindful of the foraging location, avoid areas contaminated by pollutants, such as roadsides or industrial areas, and always wash plants thoroughly to remove dirt and potential pesticides.

Wild plants require specific preparation to be safe for consumption, with some needing to be cooked to neutralize toxins. In contrast, others may only have certain edible parts. Researching and understanding the best practices for preparing each plant you intend to eat is essential. Incorporating wild plants into your diet can significantly enhance your nutritional intake, as many wild greens are rich in vitamins and minerals. However, it's essential to introduce new foods slowly and in small quantities to monitor for any adverse reactions.

While foraging can enrich your bushcraft experience, it comes with risks. Always carry a first aid kit and know how to use it. Learn to recognize the symptoms of allergic reactions and how to respond to them. Informing someone of your foraging plans and expected return is also wise, especially if venturing into remote areas.

In conclusion, foraging for edible plants offers a sustainable way to supplement your diet with nutritious food while engaging deeply with the natural environment. With the proper knowledge and respect for nature, it can be a safe and rewarding practice. As we move forward, enhancing our skills in hunting and fishing will further expand our capabilities for survival, providing additional means to secure food in the wilderness.

Hunting and Fishing for Survival

In bushcraft, procuring food through hunting and fishing is not only a skill but a necessity for survival. This section delves into the practical aspects of hunting and fishing for sustenance, emphasizing the importance of safety, nutrition, and the ethical considerations accompanying these primal activities.

Hunting in a survival situation requires a deep understanding of the local fauna, their habits, and the most humane and efficient hunting methods. It's crucial to familiarize oneself with the legalities surrounding hunting in the area, including seasons, licensing, and permissible take methods.

When hunting, always prioritize safety. This means personal safety and ensuring that your actions do not negatively impact the environment or local wildlife populations. Use weapons that you are trained and comfortable with, and always ensure a clean, ethical kill to prevent unnecessary suffering of the animal.

Nutritionally, wild game is an excellent source of lean protein, essential fats, and other nutrients. However, it's important to understand the preparation and cooking methods to preserve these nutrients while ensuring the meat is safe to consume. Different animals require different approaches to butchering and cooking, so knowledge and preparation are essential.

Similarly, fishing requires knowledge of the local aquatic species, habitats, and behaviors. Understanding the basics of sustainable fishing practices is essential to ensure that fish populations remain healthy for future generations.

When fishing for survival, consider the nutritional value of the fish you aim to catch. Fish are a rich source of omega-3 fatty acids, protein, and other vital nutrients. However, the preparation and cooking method can significantly affect their nutritional content. Aim for methods that preserve these nutrients, such as grilling or steaming rather than deep-frying.

Safety is also a paramount concern when fishing. This includes personal safety measures, such as being aware of the weather and water conditions, as well as the safety of the fish populations. Practice catch-and-release when appropriate, and be mindful of local size and bag limit regulations.

Ethics play a crucial role in hunting and fishing for survival. It's essential to approach these activities with respect for nature and the animals you're hunting or fishing. This means taking only what you need, minimizing waste, and ensuring your actions do not cause unnecessary harm or suffering.

In conclusion, hunting and fishing are invaluable skills in bushcraft and survival situations. They provide both a means of sustenance and a connection to the natural world. By approaching these activities with respect, knowledge, and preparation, one can ensure personal survival and the preservation of the natural environment and its inhabitants.

Preventing Foodborne Illnesses

The risk of foodborne illnesses increases in the wilderness, where modern food preservation and safety standards are not available. However, with the proper knowledge and precautions, these risks can be minimized, ensuring a safer and more enjoyable bushcraft experience. This section covers practical strategies for preventing foodborne illnesses by focusing on handling, preparing, and storing food in the wild.

Foodborne illnesses result from consuming contaminated food or beverages, with bacteria, viruses, parasites, or toxins being the usual culprits. Symptoms can range from mild discomfort to severe dehydration and, in extreme cases, death. In a survival situation, even a mild case can become dangerous if it leads to dehydration or impairs the ability to seek help or self-rescue.

To ensure safe food handling, washing hands and surfaces often is essential. If soap is unavailable, ash or sand can be used as alternatives. It's also crucial to keep all surfaces and utensils used for food preparation clean. To avoid cross-contamination, separate cutting boards and knives should be used for raw meat and other foods, preventing the transfer of harmful bacteria. Cooking foods to safe temperatures is another critical practice; wild game should be cooked to an internal temperature of at least 165°F (74°C), and fish should be cooked until opaque and flaky.

When it comes to food storage, keeping cold foods cold and hot foods hot is essential. Perishable foods should be kept cool using natural refrigeration methods, such as submerging items in a cold stream or burying them in a cool, shaded area. Cooked food not consumed immediately should be kept hot to prevent bacterial growth or consumed as soon as possible if heating equipment is unavailable. Drying is an effective method for long-term storage of meats, fruits, and vegetables, ensuring they are thoroughly dried to prevent mold and bacterial growth.

Recognizing and choosing safe foods is also crucial.

Correct identification is vital to avoid consuming toxic species when foraging for wild plants, fruits, or nuts. It's essential to use reliable field guides or the knowledge of experienced foragers. Similarly, caution should be exercised when selecting wild game and fish, avoiding animals that appear sick or behave abnormally and fish from polluted waters, which may carry diseases or harmful toxins.

In conclusion, preventing foodborne illnesses in the wilderness requires diligence and knowledge. Adhering to safe food handling, preparation, and storage practices can significantly reduce the risk of becoming ill. The goal is to survive and thrive in the natural environment, and maintaining good health through safe food practices is a critical component of bushcraft first aid.

Cooking and Preserving Wild Food

Understanding how to cook and preserve wild food safely is crucial in bushcraft for maintaining health and ensuring survival. This involves essential techniques and considerations for processing wild edibles, focusing on safety and nutritional preservation.

Cooking wild food enhances its flavor and is a critical step in eliminating potential pathogens. Thorough cooking of wild game, fish, or foraged plants is necessary, ensuring meats reach an internal temperature of at least 165°F (74°C) to destroy harmful bacteria like Salmonella and E. coli. Boiling plants for at least one minute can kill off most pathogens. However, some toxic plants require more specific treatment to neutralize their harmful components.

The cooking method is also essential; open fires are common in bushcraft but require careful management. Constructing a simple reflector oven from logs or rocks can help distribute heat more evenly. Using hot stones from the fire placed in a pit with the food and then covered with earth creates a makeshift oven that slowly cooks the food, preserving nutrients and reducing burning risks.

Preserving food for leaner times is a wise strategy when food is abundant. Various methods are available for preserving wild food, each with its advantages:

- **Drying** is an energy-efficient method, suitable for meat, fruits, vegetables, and herbs, especially in sunny, breezy locations or near a fire, ensuring thorough drying to prevent mold while avoiding over-drying.
- **Smoking** meat and fish preserves them and adds flavor, requiring a simple smoker setup

and a low, consistent heat to avoid under-preservation.
- **Fermenting** extends shelf life and enhances nutritional value but requires knowledge of safe practices to avoid food poisoning.
- **Salting** draws out moisture to inhibit bacterial growth, with the challenge being to use enough salt for preservation without making the food too salty, followed by drying or smoking for additional preservation.

Hygiene is paramount, emphasizing clean hands, utensils, and surfaces to minimize contamination risks. Additionally, thoroughly understanding which plants and mushrooms are safe to eat is crucial, as some remain poisonous even after cooking or preservation. Mastering these techniques ensures a reliable food source in the wilderness, significantly contributing to health and survival in bushcraft situations.

Chapter Summary

- Foraging for edible plants is a crucial survival skill, requiring knowledge of plant

identification, harvesting, and preparation to enhance food safety and nutrition.
- Misidentification of plants can lead to consuming toxic species; learning about local flora and focusing on easily recognizable plants like dandelions, nettles, and wild garlic is essential.
- Sustainable harvesting practices, such as taking no more than a third of available plants and avoiding contaminated areas, are crucial for ecosystem preservation.
- Many wild plants need specific preparation to be safe for consumption, and incorporating them into your diet can significantly improve nutritional intake.
- Hunting and fishing for survival require understanding local fauna, legalities, safety, and ethical considerations, emphasizing minimizing environmental impact and animal suffering.
- Preventing foodborne illnesses in the wilderness involves safe food handling, preparation, and storage practices, including washing hands, avoiding cross-contamination, and cooking foods to safe temperatures.

- Cooking and preserving wild food safely is paramount, and techniques like drying, smoking, fermenting, and salting are vital for eliminating pathogens and extending food's shelf life.

6

SHELTER AND EXPOSURE PROTECTION

Shelter built into a tree.

Choosing a Safe Shelter Location

In bushcraft first aid, understanding how to choose a safe shelter location is paramount for survival and protection against the elements. This decision can significantly impact your ability to maintain body heat, stay dry, and avoid potential hazards. The following guidelines are designed to help you select an optimal site for your shelter, ensuring your safety and comfort in wilderness settings.

First and foremost, look for natural protection from the elements. This could be a rock overhang, a dense stand of trees, or a depression in the ground. These features can provide essential shelter from wind, rain, and snow, reducing the need for extensive shelter construction. However, it's crucial to assess the stability of these natural shelters to avoid any risk of collapse or flooding.

Elevation is another critical factor to consider. While setting up camp in a low-lying area near a water source might seem appealing, these locations are prone to cold air pools at night, which can significantly lower the temperature. Furthermore, valleys and depressions are at a higher risk of flooding. Instead, seek out a flat spot on higher ground, ensuring it's not at the peak where you would be exposed to strong winds.

Proximity to water is essential for hydration, cooking, and hygiene. However, establishing your shelter too close to water bodies can lead to problems. Apart from the flooding risk, areas near water attract insects and wildlife. A distance of about 60-100 meters from a water source strikes a good balance between convenience and safety.

Consideration of potential hazards is crucial. Avoid areas with a risk of falling rocks or branches, which can be identified by looking for debris on the ground. Also, steer clear of animal paths to reduce the likelihood of unwanted encounters with wildlife. Inspecting the area for signs of insects, such as ant hills or wasp nests, is also advisable to prevent uncomfortable or dangerous situations.

Lastly, the orientation of your shelter can play a significant role in your comfort and survival. In colder climates, positioning the entrance away from prevailing winds while capturing morning sunlight can help warm the shelter. In warmer regions, maximizing ventilation and shade will be more beneficial to avoid overheating.

By carefully assessing these factors, you can choose a shelter location that offers safety, comfort, and protection. This strategic selection is the first step in ensuring your well-being in the wilderness, setting a solid foundation for constructing insulated shelters and other survival tactics covered in bushcraft first aid.

Building Insulated Shelters

When selecting an appropriate location for your shelter, it's crucial to ensure your safety and comfort in the wilderness by constructing a shelter that provides adequate insulation. Insulation is essential for protection against the cold, retaining body heat, and even shielding you from the heat in warmer climates. This section will help you build insulated shelters using materials commonly found in the wilderness.

First, you need to gather the materials for insulation and structure. Dry leaves, moss, pine needles, and small branches are excellent for insulation as they trap air, a poor conductor of heat, thereby retaining warmth within the shelter. For the shelter's structure, search for larger branches, fallen trees, or natural features like a rock face that can serve as the backbone of your construction.

Begin constructing your shelter by setting up the framework. If you're utilizing a fallen tree or a rock face as a base, arrange large branches at an angle to create a lean-to structure. It's essential to ensure that the framework is sturdy enough to support the weight of the insulating materials and any additional snow or debris that may accumulate.

Once the framework is established, add your

insulating materials from the bottom up, layering leaves, moss, and pine needles. The effectiveness of the insulation increases with its thickness; aim for a minimum thickness of 12 inches (30 cm) on all sides of the shelter, including the ground. Placing branches over the insulation as you progress can help keep it in place and add an extra layer of protection against the elements.

After insulating the shelter, inspect it for gaps or holes where the wind could penetrate and use additional insulating materials to fill them. The entrance of your shelter requires special attention to reduce heat loss; consider creating a small hallway or positioning the entrance away from the prevailing wind.

Before settling in for the night, test the shelter's insulation by spending a short period inside with the entrance sealed. If you notice any drafts, reinforce these areas with more insulation. The effectiveness of your shelter's insulation is crucial for a comfortable and safe night.

Maintain your shelter throughout your stay. Insulation materials may settle or compress, reducing their effectiveness. Regularly fluff up the insulation and add more materials as needed. After any wind or snow, check the shelter for damage and make necessary repairs.

Following these steps can significantly increase your comfort and safety in the wilderness. Remember, the key to effective insulation is thickness and coverage, so ensure your shelter is well-insulated on all sides, including the ground, to protect against the cold and retain body heat.

Protecting Yourself from the Elements

In the wilderness, your ability to find or create shelter is your first line of defense against the harsh elements. However, there will be times when you're exposed to the elements, either while moving between shelters or when a shelter isn't immediately available. Protecting yourself from wind, rain, snow, and sun is crucial for your survival and well-being. This involves practical strategies to shield yourself from the adverse effects of exposure.

To protect against wind, which can strip away the warm air your body maintains around itself and increase the risk of hypothermia, use natural terrain features like rocks, trees, or depressions to break the wind's force. If moving, orient your body and backpack to minimize exposure to the wind. A windbreak made from branches, a tarp, or snow can provide temporary relief.

Rain can lead to discomfort, hypothermia, or trench foot if not appropriately managed. Waterproof clothing is essential, but in its absence, a poncho or tarp can serve as a makeshift raincoat or shelter. When setting up camp, look for a location with a natural overhead cover or elevation to avoid water pooling. Keeping dry is crucial, so wring out wet clothing and dry it by a fire or in the sun whenever possible.

Snow poses a unique challenge as it can insulate and induce hypothermia. Use snow to your advantage by building a shelter like a quinzhee or snow cave for insulation. If on the move, layer your clothing to keep warm air close to your body and prevent snow from melting into your layers by waterproofing your outer layer. Avoid sweating to reduce heat loss.

Sun exposure can lead to dehydration, sunburn, and heatstroke. Protect your skin with clothing, hats, and sunscreen. Use sunglasses or improvised eyewear to prevent snow blindness in snowy environments. Seek shade during the hottest parts of the day and travel during cooler hours if necessary. A simple shade shelter can offer temporary relief during rest stops.

Several general principles apply regardless of the element you're facing. Stay hydrated and well-fed to maintain resilience against extreme temperatures. Layer your clothing to quickly adjust to changing conditions and be prepared to improvise with what you have. Your mental attitude plays a significant role in your physical well-being, so stay calm, assess your situation logically, and take decisive action to protect yourself from the elements.

Understanding and applying these strategies can significantly increase your chances of staying safe and healthy in the wilderness, even under challenging environmental conditions.

Fire Safety and Warmth

Mastering the art of creating and maintaining a fire is crucial in the wilderness, as it serves as a lifeline. Fire not only provides warmth and light but also enables the cooking of food and the purification of water and can be vital in signaling for help. Alongside its numerous benefits, it's important to practice fire safety to prevent injuries and protect the environment. This section will walk you through the essentials of safely utilizing fire's life-saving benefits.

When selecting a location for your fire, it's essential to choose a spot sheltered from the wind yet with good ventilation to prevent smoke inhalation. Avoid areas close to trees, bushes, and other flammable materials to reduce the risk of the fire spreading. Clear a wide area on the soil, removing any leaves, twigs, and debris that could catch fire. If possible, use a fire pit surrounded by rocks to help contain the fire.

Before lighting your fire, you must gather three materials: tinder, kindling, and fuel. Tinder includes small, easily ignitable items such as dry leaves, grass, or twigs. Kindling consists of slightly larger sticks that can catch fire from the tinder, and fuel is made up of larger pieces of wood that will keep the fire burning for longer. Arrange these materials nearby so they can be added to the fire as needed, but ensure they are not so close as to catch fire from a stray spark.

Always opt for a safe ignition source for lighting the fire, like matches or a lighter. In damp conditions, waterproof matches or a fire starter may be necessary. Avoid using flammable liquids such as gasoline, as they can lead to uncontrollable flames and serious injuries. Begin by lighting the tinder and then gently add kindling as the fire grows, followed by the larger pieces of fuel. Keeping the fire manageable is essential to meet your needs without becoming a hazard.

To maintain your fire, add fuel as needed, but ensure it doesn't grow too large. Always have water or soil on hand to extinguish the fire if necessary. It's crucial never to leave your fire unattended, as a sudden gust of wind could cause the flames to spread. When extinguishing the fire, do so gradually by sprinkling water or covering it with soil, then stir the ashes to make sure no embers remain that could reignite.

Despite taking all precautions, accidents can happen, and burns may occur. Cool the area with clean water for minor burns, and cover it with a sterile dressing. Seek medical attention immediately for more severe burns. Always keep a first aid kit nearby when handling fire.

Lastly, it's important to practice Leave No Trace principles to minimize the impact of your fire on the environment. Use existing fire rings when available and ensure your fire is completely extinguished and cold to the touch before leaving the site. To further reduce impact, scatter cool ashes over a wide area away from the campsite.

By adhering to these guidelines, you can enjoy the numerous benefits of a fire while ensuring your safety and the protection of the wilderness. Fire is a powerful tool in bushcraft and survival but requires respect and responsibility.

Chapter Summary

- Choose a shelter site with natural cover, such as rock overhangs or dense trees, on high ground away from water to prevent flooding, and position it to suit the climate.
- Build the shelter using dry leaves, moss, and branches for insulation, aiming for at least 12 inches of thickness for warmth and sealing gaps against the wind.
- Use the landscape and items like tarps to shield against wind, rain, and snow, and wear appropriate clothing and sunscreen for sun protection.
- For fire safety, pick a sheltered, airy spot away from flammables, prepare with tinder, kindling, and fuel, keep the fire small, and ensure it's fully extinguished afterward.
- Maintain hydration and nutrition, adjust clothing layers for temperature, use what's available for improvisation, and stay calm and logical in problem-solving.
- Follow Leave No Trace principles to minimize environmental impact, use existing fire rings, and scatter cooled ashes.

- Survival hinges on good insulation, element protection, fire safety, and effective signaling, highlighting the importance of preparation, improvisation, and environmental respect.

7

NAVIGATING MENTAL HEALTH CHALLENGES

An adventurer dealing with stress in the wilderness.

Coping with Stress and Anxiety

In the wilderness, where the unpredictability of nature meets the solitude of the untamed, stress and anxiety can become as challenging as any physical obstacle. The key to coping with these mental health challenges lies in understanding their roots and employing practical strategies to mitigate their impact.

First and foremost, it's essential to recognize the signs of stress and anxiety. These can manifest in various ways, including increased heart rate, restlessness, difficulty concentrating, and irritability. Acknowledging these symptoms early on is the first step towards managing them effectively.

Establishing a routine is one effective strategy for coping with stress and anxiety in bushcraft situations. The wilderness's unpredictability can be overwhelming, but a routine provides a sense of control and normalcy. This could be as simple as setting up camp before dusk, gathering water at dawn, or allocating specific meal times. Such predictability can be a comforting anchor amid chaos.

Another vital technique is mindfulness and grounding exercises. When anxiety strikes, grounding oneself in the present moment can help mitigate overwhelming feelings. Techniques such as deep breathing, mindfulness meditation, or even focusing on the sensory experiences of the wilderness (the sound of a nearby stream, the smell of pine, the feel of the earth beneath your feet) can help calm the mind and reduce anxiety levels.

Physical activity is also a powerful tool for managing stress and anxiety. Bushcraft inherently involves physical tasks, but it's important to engage in these activities mindfully, focusing on the movement and the environment rather than as a mere survival chore. This not only helps expend pent-up energy but also boosts endorphin levels, improving mood and reducing stress.

Even in a solitary bushcraft scenario, social support should be considered. Open communication about feelings and experiences can provide a sense of shared understanding and support if you're with a group. If you're alone, keeping a journal or speaking aloud about your thoughts and feelings can offer a form of emotional release and reflection.

Lastly, setting realistic goals and celebrating small achievements can significantly boost morale. In a bushcraft context, this could mean successfully starting a fire with damp wood, finding a water source, or building a shelter that withstands the night. These achievements provide tangible evidence of progress and capability, which can be incredibly uplifting in moments of doubt.

In conclusion, coping with stress and anxiety in

bushcraft requires a multifaceted approach that encompasses physical, emotional, and psychological strategies. By recognizing the signs, establishing routines, practicing mindfulness, engaging in physical activity, seeking social support, and celebrating small victories, one can navigate the mental challenges of the wilderness with resilience and grace.

The Psychological Impact of Survival Situations

Survival situations exert a profound psychological impact on individuals. The stress of navigating the unknown, coupled with the physical demands of bushcraft, can significantly affect one's mental health. Understanding this impact is crucial for anyone venturing into the wilderness, as it is the first step toward maintaining psychological well-being in challenging environments.

The initial reaction to a survival situation often involves a surge of adrenaline. This fight-or-flight response can provide the necessary energy to deal with immediate threats. However, this state could be more sustainable in the long term. Once the initial shock wears off, the reality of the situation sets in, and individuals may experience a wide range of emotions, including fear, anxiety, frustration, and despair. These feelings are natural responses to wilderness survival's uncertainty and potential dangers.

One of the most significant psychological impacts of survival situations is the sense of loss of control. People are accustomed to having a certain degree of control over their environment and outcomes in everyday life. In the wilderness, however, many variables are beyond one's control, such as weather conditions, availability of resources, and potential hazards. This loss of control can lead to feelings of helplessness and vulnerability, which, if not addressed, can escalate into more severe mental health issues, such as depression or acute stress disorder.

Moreover, the isolation often experienced in survival scenarios can exacerbate these psychological challenges. Humans are inherently social creatures; lacking social interaction can lead to loneliness and disconnection. This isolation can hinder one's ability to maintain a positive outlook. It can impair decision-making abilities, as no one can discuss options or strategies with.

To mitigate these psychological impacts, it is essential to develop coping strategies that can help maintain mental resilience. Simple techniques, such as setting small, achievable goals, practicing mindfulness, and focusing on the tasks, can provide a sense of control and purpose. Additionally, even in the wilderness, maintaining a routine can offer a semblance of normalcy and stability, comforting in times of stress.

Acknowledging and accepting the emotions that arise in survival situations is also essential. Suppressing or denying feelings of fear or anxiety can lead to increased stress and mental fatigue. Instead, recognizing these emotions as natural responses to the circumstances allows individuals to address them constructively by adjusting their approach to the situation or using relaxation techniques to manage stress.

In conclusion, the psychological impact of survival situations is a critical aspect of bushcraft first aid that requires as much attention as physical injuries. By understanding the mental challenges that may arise and equipping oneself with strategies to cope with them, individuals can enhance their resilience and improve their chances of surviving and thriving in the wilderness. The journey through the mental landscape of survival is as demanding as the physical trek. Still, with the proper preparation and mindset, it is possible to navigate this terrain successfully.

Building Resilience and Mental Toughness

Understanding the psychological impact of survival situations is crucial, as is developing the resilience and mental toughness needed to navigate these challenges effectively. It's not just about enduring; it's about adapting and thriving in adversity. Practical strategies and techniques to fortify mental resilience are essential for anyone venturing into the wilderness or engaging in bushcraft activities.

A positive mindset is fundamental to resilience, focusing on solutions rather than problems and viewing challenges as opportunities for growth. Practicing gratitude by acknowledging what you are thankful for daily, even in difficult situations, can shift your focus from what's lacking to what's abundant, fostering a more positive outlook.

Setting achievable goals provides direction and a sense of purpose, such as building a shelter or finding water in a survival situation. Achieving these goals boosts morale and motivates you to tackle the next challenge.

Stress is inevitable, but maintaining mental toughness is critical. Techniques like deep breathing, meditation, and mindfulness can calm the mind and reduce anxiety, preparing you to handle stress more effectively when it arises.

Problem-solving is a critical resilience skill. It involves identifying problems, brainstorming solutions, evaluating them, and implementing the most viable ones. Practicing problem-solving can make you more adept at handling unexpected challenges.

A robust support system provides emotional strength and encouragement, offering valuable insights and coping strategies. In survival contexts, working effectively as a team enhances problem-solving capabilities and provides mutual support.

Resilience involves learning from failure and viewing each setback as an opportunity to grow. Reflecting on what went wrong and how to improve turns failure from a discouragement source into a stepping stone toward success.

Physical and mental resilience are interconnected; regular exercise improves health, reduces stress, and enhances mental toughness. Incorporating physical training into preparation for bushcraft activities can significantly bolster resilience.

Visualizing yourself successfully navigating challenges, a technique known as mental rehearsal, prepares your mind for the challenges ahead, making you more confident and resilient. Building resilience and mental toughness is a continuous process that requires practice and dedication.

By incorporating these strategies into your preparation and mindset, you can enhance your ability to navigate the mental health challenges of survival situations, ensuring your survival and your ability to thrive in the face of adversity.

Chapter Summary

- Recognize signs of stress and anxiety in wilderness situations, such as increased heart rate and difficulty concentrating.
- Establish a routine to provide a sense of control and normalcy amidst the unpredictability of the wilderness.
- To mitigate anxiety, practice mindfulness and grounding exercises like deep breathing and focusing on sensory experiences.
- Exercise to manage stress, boost endorphins, and improve mood.
- Seek social support through open communication or journaling to share feelings and experiences.

- Set realistic goals and celebrate small achievements to boost morale and provide evidence of progress.
- Maintain morale and hope by establishing routines, setting achievable goals, and staying connected with nature.
- Build resilience and mental toughness through cultivating a positive mindset, managing stress, developing problem-solving skills, and learning from failure.

8

EMERGENCY SIGNALING AND RESCUE

A man lighting a flare in the wilderness.

Creating Effective Signals

In bushcraft and wilderness survival, creating effective signals for rescue is paramount. This skill can significantly increase your chances of being found by rescuers in an emergency. The key to successful signaling lies in understanding and utilizing three primary principles: visibility, audibility, and repetition.

Visibility is your foremost ally in the wilderness. To create obvious signals, consider using bright colors, especially those that starkly contrast the natural environment. For instance, orange, red, and neon colors are particularly effective. One method is to use a brightly colored fabric or an emergency blanket to create a large, noticeable sign on the ground or to hang it from a tree. The international distress signal, which consists of three of anything (three fires, three piles of rocks, and three pieces of fabric), is a universally recognized sign for help. Arranging these signals in an open area can enhance their visibility from the air.

Reflective materials can also play a crucial role in signaling for help. Mirrors or any reflective surface can catch the sun's rays and signal to aircraft. The key is to aim the reflection toward the potential rescuer, using the "flash" of light to grab attention. This method requires sunlight, so it's essential to consider the time of day and weather conditions when planning to use this technique.

Audibility complements visibility in emergency signaling. Sound can be your best signaling tool in environments where visibility is limited, such as dense forests or at night. Whistles are excellent for this purpose as they can produce a loud, piercing sound that can travel long distances. Three blasts of a whistle, repeated at regular intervals, is a recognized distress signal. Banging metal objects together or using a horn can also create effective auditory signals.

Repetition is the third principle of effective signaling. A signal is more likely to be noticed if repeated at regular intervals. This applies to both visual and auditory signals. For visual signals, ensure they are maintained and visible until rescue arrives. For auditory signals, set a schedule for producing the sound, such as every hour, to increase the chances of being heard by rescuers.

Remember, creating effective signals aims to make it as easy as possible for rescuers to locate you. Applying these principles can significantly improve your chances of a successful rescue in an emergency. Always be prepared to use whatever materials you have at your disposal and think creatively to enhance the effectiveness of your signals.

Using Technology for Rescue

In the wilderness, where the beauty of nature meets the unpredictability of outdoor adventures, the importance of preparedness cannot be overstated. While traditional signaling methods play a crucial role in emergencies, technology has introduced a new layer of safety and efficiency in rescue operations. This section delves into the use of technology for rescue, providing practical advice on how to leverage modern devices and services to ensure your safety in the great outdoors.

Personal Locator Beacons (PLBs): A Personal Locator Beacon is a compact device designed to send an SOS signal to your location to search and rescue services. When activated, a PLB transmits a distress signal to the nearest search and rescue satellite system, relaying your position and information to local search and rescue teams. It's essential for adventurers venturing into remote areas where cell service is nonexistent. Ensure your PLB is registered with your details for a swift response in an emergency.

Satellite Messengers: These devices offer two-way communication capabilities, allowing you to send and receive text messages via satellite networks. In addition to SOS functions similar to PLBs, satellite messengers enable you to communicate with family, friends, or emergency services, even from the most remote locations. Some models also allow for weather updates and navigation features, making them a versatile tool for bushcraft enthusiasts.

Smartphone Apps: In areas with cellular coverage, several smartphone applications can enhance your safety. Apps designed for outdoor adventures can provide GPS navigation, weather alerts, and even the ability to share your real-time location with trusted contacts. While relying solely on a smartphone is not advisable due to battery life constraints and potential lack of signal, these apps can be valuable to your safety toolkit when used appropriately.

Emergency Signal Mirrors and Whistles: Though not electronic, these tools are worth mentioning for their simplicity and effectiveness in conjunction with technology. Under the right conditions, an emergency signal mirror can catch the attention of rescuers from miles away, while a whistle can be heard over long distances when visibility is poor or in densely wooded areas. Both items should be a staple in any bushcraft first aid kit as a backup to your technological devices.

Preparation and Practice: Regardless of the technology you choose to carry, familiarizing yourself with its operation before embarking on your adventure is crucial. Practice using your devices in various conditions to ensure you can operate them effectively in an emergency. Additionally, inform someone of your planned route and expected return time, providing them with instructions on what to do if you fail to check-in.

In conclusion, integrating technology into your bushcraft first aid and rescue toolkit offers a significant advantage in ensuring safety and facilitating rescue in emergencies. By combining traditional signaling methods with modern technology, you can enjoy the wilderness with the confidence that help is within reach should you need it. As we move forward, the next section will guide you through navigational aids and techniques, further equipping you with the knowledge to navigate the wilderness safely and efficiently.

Navigational Aids and Techniques

In bushcraft and wilderness survival, effectively navigating through the wilderness is not just a skill—it's essential for survival. Beyond the basic knowledge of using a map and compass, numerous navigational aids and techniques can significantly improve your chances of being rescued or finding your way back to safety. This section explores these vital tools and methods, aiming to equip you with the skills needed to navigate emergencies in the wilderness.

Wilderness Lifeline

Nature offers various navigational aids for those who know how to interpret them. The sun, stars, and even the growth patterns of moss on trees can provide directional clues. For example, in the Northern Hemisphere, the sun's path from east to west can help establish an east-west orientation. At the same time, the North Star (Polaris) indicates north at night. These natural indicators are invaluable in the absence of compasses or GPS devices.

Another helpful skill is creating an improvised compass. This can be done by magnetizing a needle by rubbing it against silk or wool and then floating it on a leaf in still water. The needle will align with the Earth's magnetic field, indicating the north-south line. Although more accurate than a standard compass, this method can offer a crucial directional reference when needed.

Understanding how to read topographical maps is also crucial. These maps show paths and roads and detail the terrain, including hills, valleys, and bodies of water. Learning to interpret contour lines and symbols can aid in navigating through challenging landscapes and identifying potential locations for rescue signals. Combining map knowledge with land navigation skills, such as triangulation using visible landmarks, can significantly improve your ability to move purposefully toward safety or to signal for help effectively.

The importance of GPS devices and satellite messengers in navigation cannot be overstated. These tools provide precise location data, making it easier for rescuers to find you. Many of these devices also allow sending distress signals and messages from remote locations where traditional communication methods are ineffective.

Marking your path when moving is crucial for helping rescuers track your movements and preventing you from circling back on yourself. Creating noticeable but environmentally friendly markers using natural materials, as well as understanding how to leave clear, universal distress signals, can facilitate search teams' efforts to locate you.

A key aspect of navigation is not just finding your way but also "staying found." This involves making informed decisions about when to move and when to stay put to increase your visibility to rescuers. Establishing a visible campsite, using bright materials, or creating smoke signals can make it easier for search teams to find you.

In conclusion, mastering navigational aids and techniques is critical to bushcraft first aid and emergency preparedness. From recognizing natural cues to leveraging modern technology, these skills enable confident navigation through the wilderness. As we move forward, the focus will shift to effectively interacting with rescuers, ensuring that once found, you can communicate your needs and understand their instructions, completing the rescue process efficiently and safely.

Interacting with Rescuers

Interacting with rescuers is critical in any survival situation in the wilderness. After successfully signaling for help using the techniques and navigational aids discussed, the focus shifts to ensuring a safe and effective handover to the rescue team. This section delves into the best practices for interacting with rescuers, emphasizing clear communication, understanding rescue operations, and preparing for evacuation.

First and foremost, it's vital to remain visible and make it easy for rescuers to reach you. If you've used signals to attract attention, maintain those signals as long as possible or until rescuers signal you to stop. This could mean burning a fire, leaving a signal mirror in a visible location, or using signaling devices.

Once rescuers are in sight, follow their instructions

carefully. They may guide you verbally or use hand signals, especially if they are approaching from a helicopter and the noise makes communication difficult. If you're in a group, designate one person to communicate with the rescuers to avoid confusion.

It's also important to inform the rescuers of any medical emergencies or injuries within your group. Be prepared to quickly and accurately describe the nature of the injuries, any first aid administered, and the current condition of the injured party. This information is crucial for rescuers to prioritize medical attention and allocate resources effectively.

It is essential to understand that rescue operations may take time to set up, especially in challenging terrain. Rescuers must assess the situation, possibly secure the area, and determine the safest extraction method. During this time, remain calm, stay in place unless instructed otherwise, and keep your group together.

Preparing for evacuation involves several key steps. Gather all your gear and be ready to move on short notice. If there are injured individuals, ensure they are as comfortable and stable as possible for transport. Listen to the rescuers' instructions on assisting in the evacuation process, whether that involves helping to carry the injured, following a

Wilderness Lifeline

specific path, or boarding a rescue vehicle in an orderly manner.

Lastly, once you are in the care of the rescue team, trust their expertise and follow their guidance. They are trained professionals equipped to handle wilderness rescues. They will take the necessary steps to ensure your safety and well-being.

Interacting with rescuers effectively can significantly impact the outcome of a rescue operation. By staying visible, communicating clearly, and following instructions, you can aid in a smooth and efficient rescue process, paving the way for a safe evacuation from the wilderness.

Preparing for Evacuation

In the wilderness, the moment you realize that evacuation is necessary, whether due to injury, severe weather, or any other critical situation, your preparation for a safe extraction begins. This preparation is a multifaceted process that involves both physical and mental readiness, ensuring that when rescuers arrive, you are ready to leave promptly and safely.

1. Gather Essential Items: Assemble a small, lightweight pack of essential items. This should include a first aid kit, personal medication, a water bottle, high-energy food bars, a flashlight or headlamp with extra batteries, a whistle, a compact emergency blanket, and a multi-tool. If possible, include a copy of your identification and any relevant medical information. This pack should be easily accessible and ready to grab at a moment's notice.

2. Mark Your Location: While waiting for rescue, make your location visible from the air and ground. Use bright materials or reflective items, or create signals on the ground using rocks or logs that contrast with the natural environment. If you have a fire, consider creating smoke signals by adding green vegetation to the fire to produce thick smoke during the day. At night, a fire itself can be a powerful signal.

3. Prepare Physically and Mentally: Depending on the nature of the emergency, physical preparation might involve dressing appropriately for the weather or terrain, staying hydrated and nourished, or administering first aid to yourself or others. Mental preparation is equally important. Stay calm, maintain a positive outlook, and mentally rehearse what you will say and do when rescuers arrive. This includes knowing your location as precisely as possible, understanding the nature of your emergency, and being able to communicate any immediate medical needs.

4. Secure Your Immediate Surroundings: Ensure

your immediate area is safe and accessible for rescuers. This might involve clearing a landing zone for a helicopter, marking a clear path to your location if in a dense forest, or making sure that the area around you is stable and not prone to sudden flooding, rockslides, or other hazards.

5. Conserve Your Phone Battery: If you have a cell phone with you, conserve its battery life as much as possible. Turn off non-essential apps, reduce screen brightness, and switch to airplane mode when not in use. Your phone could be your lifeline to communicate with rescuers, especially if you can send GPS coordinates or other critical information.

6. Stay Put Unless Necessary: Once you have signaled for help and are awaiting rescue, it's generally best to stay in your current location unless you have a good reason to move. Moving can make it harder for rescuers to find you, especially if you leave after signaling your location. If you must move, leave clear, unmistakable signs of your direction of travel.

7. Be Ready to Assist Rescuers: When rescuers arrive, be prepared to follow their instructions immediately. They may require your assistance in making the evacuation smoother or faster, such as by helping to carry equipment or moving to a more accessible location for extraction.

By meticulously preparing for evacuation, you increase your chances of a successful rescue and contribute to the operation's safety and efficiency. Remember, your preparation can significantly impact the outcome, so take these steps seriously and ensure you are as ready as possible when help arrives.

Chapter Summary

- Effective emergency signaling in wilderness survival relies on visibility, audibility, and repetition, using bright colors, loud sounds, and repeated signals to attract rescuers.
- Brightly colored fabrics, reflective materials, and the international distress signal of three of anything (fires, rocks, fabrics) enhance visibility for aerial rescue.
- Auditory signals like whistle blasts, banging metal objects, or using a horn can complement visual signals, especially in low-visibility conditions.
- Personal Locator Beacons (PLBs) and Satellite Messengers are crucial for sending SOS signals and enabling two-way

communication in remote areas without cell service.
- Smartphone apps can provide GPS navigation, weather alerts, and real-time location sharing. Still, they should not be solely relied upon due to battery and signal limitations.
- Essential preparation steps include familiarity with device operation, informing someone of your route and expected return, and carrying non-electronic signaling tools like mirrors and whistles.
- Navigational skills, including using natural cues, improvised compasses, topographical maps, and path marking, are vital for moving toward safety or enhancing signal visibility.
- Preparing for evacuation involves gathering essential items, making your location visible, conserving phone battery, and being ready to assist rescuers for a smooth and efficient rescue operation.

9

WEATHER AND ENVIRONMENTAL HAZARDS

Rainy weather in the wilderness.

Understanding Weather Patterns

In bushcraft, a profound understanding of weather patterns is a cornerstone for ensuring safety and preparedness in the wilderness. With its inherent unpredictability and potential for rapid change, weather poses a significant environmental hazard that can impact health, safety, and the ability to navigate or remain in the wilderness. This section delves into the critical aspects of weather patterns, equipping you with the knowledge to anticipate and respond to various environmental conditions.

Weather patterns, fundamentally, are the varying atmospheric conditions that occur over some time in a particular area. These patterns range from clear skies and mild temperatures to severe storms and extreme temperatures. Recognizing the signs of changing weather can differentiate between a successful outing and a potentially dangerous situation.

First and foremost, understanding the basics of weather systems is essential. High and low-pressure systems, fronts, and other meteorological terms are not just for forecasters but are crucial for anyone venturing into the wilderness. High-pressure systems typically bring fair weather, while low-pressure systems can lead to poor weather, including storms and rain. Recognizing the signs of these systems can give you a heads-up before changes occur.

Cloud formations and types offer significant clues about impending weather. For instance, cumulonimbus clouds are often harbingers of thunderstorms. In contrast, high and wispy cirrus clouds may indicate a change in the weather within the next 24 hours. Understanding these patterns allows for better planning and decision-making while in the bush.

Wind direction and speed can also provide insights into upcoming weather. Sudden changes in wind direction or an increase in wind speed can signify a change in weather patterns, potentially heralding the approach of a storm. By paying attention to the wind, you can often anticipate shifts in weather that could impact your activities.

Temperature fluctuations, especially sudden drops, can indicate the approach of colder weather or a storm front. Being attuned to these changes is vital, especially when considering the risks of hypothermia or other cold-related conditions in the wilderness.

Barometric pressure, measured by a barometer, is another critical tool for understanding weather patterns. A falling barometer indicates worsening weather, while a rising barometer suggests improving conditions. This tool can be invaluable for predicting weather changes quickly, allowing for timely adjustments to plans and activities.

Finally, the natural world itself provides cues about the weather. Animals, insects, and plants exhibit behavior changes that can signal weather changes. Birds flying low, for instance, can indicate bad weather approaching, as can the increased activity of ants or bees.

In summary, a comprehensive understanding of weather patterns is indispensable for anyone engaging in bushcraft. By becoming familiar with the signs and signals of changing weather, you can make informed decisions that enhance your safety and enjoyment of the wilderness. This knowledge prepares you for the challenges of the environment. It deepens your connection with nature, allowing for a more harmonious and respectful interaction with the wild.

Preparing for Extreme Weather Conditions

In bushcraft, being prepared for extreme weather conditions is crucial for comfort, survival, and safety. The unpredictability of weather, especially in wilderness areas, can quickly transform an adventure into a problematic situation. Practical strategies and essential knowledge are vital to navigate these conditions effectively.

Extreme weather can take various forms, such as severe storms, extreme heat, freezing temperatures, and sudden weather changes, each presenting unique challenges. Severe storms may cause flooding and falling trees, extreme heat can lead to dehydration and heatstroke, and freezing temperatures increase the risk of hypothermia and frostbite.

The right gear acts as the first line of defense against extreme weather. Clothing should be versatile, allowing for layering to adjust to changing conditions. Investing in quality, weather-appropriate clothing that adheres to layering principles—base layers for moisture management, insulating layers for warmth, and outer layers for wind and water protection—is essential. Carrying a well-constructed, all-weather shelter, such as a tarp or a bivvy sack, can be crucial in unexpected conditions.

Choosing the right camp location is also critical. Avoid low-lying areas that could flood during heavy rains and seek natural shelters against strong winds. In hot conditions, prioritize shade and airflow; in cold environments, seek protection from the wind. Knowing how to construct and where to place emergency shelters can significantly enhance your safety in adverse conditions.

Maintaining hydration and energy is vital in extreme weather. Increase water intake in hot weather to avoid dehydration and up your calorie intake in cold conditions as your body uses more energy to stay warm.

Always carry a means to purify water and have a reliable method to melt snow if necessary.

Monitoring the health of yourself and your companions is crucial. Be aware of the signs of hypothermia, heatstroke, dehydration, and frostbite. A well-stocked first aid kit tailored to the environment and your group's needs is essential, as is proficiency in its use to prevent minor issues from becoming life-threatening.

Advanced planning and weather awareness are essential. Research the weather patterns of your destination and be prepared for unexpected changes. It is also beneficial to develop the skill to read natural weather indicators, such as cloud formations, wind direction, and temperature shifts.

Lastly, the importance of training and continuous skills development must be considered. Attending courses, practicing regularly, and seeking to learn more about surviving in extreme weather conditions are crucial. Knowledge and preparation are your best tools in the wilderness, significantly increasing your safety and enjoyment outdoors. The goal is to survive and thrive, regardless of the challenges posed by Mother Nature.

Avoiding Natural Hazards

In the wilderness, the unpredictability of nature often presents a variety of hazards that can pose significant risks to your health and safety. Understanding how to avoid these natural hazards is crucial for any bushcraft enthusiast. Practical strategies and knowledge are essential for navigating through and mitigating the risks posed by environmental hazards.

Rivers, lakes, and streams are vital water sources but can also be treacherous. Before crossing any body of water, it's essential to continually assess the current, depth, and potential obstacles. Using a stick to gauge depth and stability can be helpful.

When crossing a river, it is advisable to choose a wide, shallow section and face upstream, leaning slightly into the current for stability. Being informed about local weather conditions and avoiding camping in flood-prone zones can help you avoid flash floods, especially in canyons and low-lying areas.

Navigating rugged terrain and dense vegetation can be challenging and may conceal potential dangers. Maintaining a steady pace and using a stick or machete to clear a path if necessary can help. It's also important to be mindful of hidden obstacles like holes, sharp rocks, and thorny plants that can cause injuries.

Wearing high boots and thick trousers can offer additional protection in areas known for snakes or other dangerous wildlife.

Encounters with wildlife can be thrilling but sometimes dangerous. Educating yourself about the local fauna and learning how to react in the event of an encounter is crucial. Making noise while hiking can help avoid surprising bears, and avoiding sudden movements is important when encountering snakes. Securing your food correctly is essential to avoid attracting animals to your campsite.

Sudden weather changes can expose you to hypothermia, heatstroke, and lightning strikes. Dressing in layers to adapt to changing temperatures and always carrying waterproof gear are good practices. In hot weather, staying hydrated, seeking shade during the hottest part of the day, and recognizing the signs of heat-related illnesses are important.

If caught in a thunderstorm, avoid open fields, high ground, and tall, isolated trees. It is advisable to find shelter in a low area but avoid depressions that can quickly fill with water.

While fire is a crucial survival tool, it's also a potential hazard. Essential safety measures include:

- Establishing a clear perimeter around your fire.
- Being free from flammable materials.
- Keeping fires manageable.
- Never leave them unattended.

Before leaving your campsite, extinguishing the fire with water and stirring the ashes is necessary.

Adopting these practices can significantly reduce the risks of natural hazards in the wilderness. The key to safely enjoying bushcraft lies in surviving and thriving through a deep understanding and respect for nature's power and unpredictability.

Surviving in Different Climates

Surviving in different climates requires a comprehensive understanding of each environment's unique challenges and hazards. Preparedness and knowledge are your best safety tools, whether in the sweltering heat of a desert, the unpredictable conditions of a rainforest, or the extreme cold of arctic regions.

Hydration is crucial in hot and dry climates as your body loses fluids quickly through sweat, leading to rapid dehydration. Always carry ample water and know how to locate and purify additional sources. Protect your skin and eyes from harmful UV rays by wearing long sleeves, hats, and sunglasses and applying sunscreen. Limit physical exertion during the hottest parts of the day by finding shade or creating a shelter to rest in until temperatures drop. Be aware of heat exhaustion and heatstroke signs, such as headache, dizziness, muscle cramps, and nausea, and take immediate steps for cooling and hydration.

For cold climates, wearing multiple layers helps trap body heat. Focus on materials that retain their insulating properties, like wool or synthetic fibers, even when wet. Staying dry is crucial to avoid hypothermia, so keep your clothing, especially socks, and gloves, dry and be mindful of sweat. Understand the early signs of frostbite, including numbness and pale or hardened skin, and protect extremities with gloves and thick socks. Increase your food intake as your body burns more calories to stay warm in cold environments.

Staying dry is essential in wet and humid climates to avoid hypothermia, even in warm environments. Use waterproof gear and seek shelter during heavy rain. Protect against insects, which are more prevalent and can carry diseases, by using insect repellent and wearing long sleeves and pants. Guard against fungal infections by keeping your skin dry and clean and changing into dry clothes immediately. Always purify water before drinking to avoid waterborne illnesses, as water sources may be abundant but contaminated.

General tips for all climates include familiarizing yourself with basic first aid techniques, such as treating cuts, burns, and bites, and carrying a well-stocked first aid kit. Navigation skills are crucial, so know how to use a compass and map to avoid disorientation. Have the means to signal for help, like a whistle, mirror, or flare; in some situations, a fire can also serve as a signal.

Understanding and respecting the unique challenges of different climates can significantly increase one's chances of surviving and thriving in the wilderness. Preparedness, adaptability, and a calm, informed approach to challenges will serve one well in any environment.

Minimizing Environmental Impact

Understanding how to navigate and endure various weather conditions and environmental hazards is paramount in bushcraft and outdoor survival. However, equally important is our responsibility to minimize our impact on these natural environments. As we venture into the wilderness, it's crucial to adopt practices that preserve the integrity and beauty of these areas for future generations.

One of the fundamental principles of minimizing environmental impact is the concept of Leave No Trace. This approach entails leaving the environment as you found it, or even better, by not leaving any physical evidence of your presence. This can be achieved through several practical measures:

Campsite Selection: Choose a campsite on durable surfaces such as established trails and campsites, rock, gravel, dry grasses, or snow. Avoid altering sites, moving rocks, or vegetation. Camping at least 200 feet from lakes and streams also helps protect riparian areas.

Waste Disposal: Pack out all trash, leftover food, and litter. Utilize catholes (6-8 inches deep) dug at least 200 feet from water sources, camps, and trails for human waste. Cover and disguise the cathole when finished. For washing yourself or your dishes, carry water 200 feet away from streams or lakes and use small amounts of biodegradable soap.

Minimizing Campfire Impacts: Where fires are permitted, use established fire rings, pans, or mound fires. Keep fires small, using only sticks from the ground that can be broken by hand. Burn all wood and coals to ash, put out campfires completely, then scatter cool ashes.

Leave What You Find: Preserve the past by leaving rocks, plants, archaeological artifacts, and other natural objects as you find them. Clean gear and boots before and after your trip to avoid introducing or transporting non-native species.

Wildlife Respect: Observe wildlife from a distance. Do not follow or approach them. Never feed animals, as feeding wildlife damages their health, alters natural behaviors, and exposes them to predators and other dangers.

Minimize Campfire Use: Consider alternatives to fires, such as a lightweight stove for cooking and a lantern for light. Use established fire rings or make a mound fire if you must have a fire.

Be Considerate of Other Visitors: Respect other visitors and protect the quality of their experience. Be courteous. Yield to other users on the trail. Let nature's sounds prevail. Avoid loud voices and noises.

By adhering to these practices, bushcraft enthusiasts ensure their safety and enjoyment and contribute to the conservation of these precious environments. It's a shared responsibility to protect natural habitats, ensuring they remain vibrant and accessible for outdoor adventurers now and in the future. Through mindful actions and a commitment to sustainability, we can all play a part in preserving the wilderness for its intrinsic value and the enjoyment of future generations.

Chapter Summary

- Understanding weather patterns is crucial for safety and preparedness in bushcraft, as it allows one to anticipate and respond to environmental conditions.
- Knowledge of weather systems, cloud formations, wind direction, temperature fluctuations, and barometric pressure is essential for predicting weather changes.
- Natural cues from animals, insects, and plants can also indicate impending weather changes.
- Preparing for extreme weather involves understanding risks, having the right gear, choosing safe shelter locations, staying hydrated, monitoring health, and planning.
- Avoiding natural hazards in the wilderness includes being cautious around water bodies, navigating through challenging terrain and vegetation, managing encounters with

wildlife, and being prepared for weather extremes and fire safety.
- Surviving in different climates requires specific strategies for hydration, sun protection, clothing layers, staying dry, and managing food intake to adapt to hot, cold, wet, and humid conditions.
- It is crucial to minimize environmental impact while engaging in bushcraft and outdoor survival, following Leave No Trace principles to preserve natural environments for future generations.
- Practices for minimizing impact include careful campsite selection, proper waste disposal, minimizing campfire impacts, respecting wildlife, and considering other visitors.

10

ADVANCED FIRST AID TECHNIQUES

Crutches made from sticks in the wilderness.

Suturing Wounds in the Field

In the wilderness, where medical facilities are often miles away, the ability to manage injuries effectively can be life-saving. Suturing is one such skill, particularly for deep or gaping wounds that cannot be closed with bandages alone. This section delves into the essentials of suturing wounds in the field, which requires both knowledge and caution.

Before considering suturing, it's crucial to assess the wound thoroughly. Suturing is appropriate for clean, sharp cuts that are too large to heal correctly. However, puncture wounds, animal bites, or any injuries showing signs of infection should not be sutured closed due to the risk of trapping bacteria inside.

Once you've determined a wound is a candidate for suturing, the next step is ensuring you have the proper tools. A suture kit typically includes sterile needles, thread, scissors, forceps, and antiseptic solution. You might need access to a pre-packaged suture kit in an improvised bushcraft situation. If you must improvise, prioritize sterilization. Needles and thread can be sterilized by boiling them in water or using a flame. However, the latter method requires caution to avoid weakening the material.

Sterilizing the wound and the surrounding skin is equally important. Use an antiseptic solution if available; otherwise, clean, boiled water cooled to a safe temperature can suffice. The goal is to minimize the risk of infection, which can complicate the healing process significantly.

The technique for suturing is delicate and requires practice. Begin by threading the needle and tying a knot at the end of the thread. Use forceps to bring the edges of the wound together gently. Insert the needle through the skin about a quarter-inch from the edge of the wound, ensuring the stitch encompasses both sides of the wound for even closure. The stitches should be spaced about a quarter-inch apart for optimal healing. After completing the suturing, tie off the final stitch securely.

In the days following suturing, it's imperative to monitor the wound closely. Signs of infection, such as increased redness, swelling, warmth, or pus, necessitate immediate attention. If these symptoms arise, the sutures may need to be removed for proper cleaning and drainage.

Finally, understanding when to remove the sutures is as essential as knowing how to place them. Generally, sutures on the face can be removed in about 3-5 days, while those on areas where the skin is under tension, such as the joints, might need to stay in place for up to 10 days. Continually assess the wound's healing progress before deciding to remove sutures.

Suturing is a valuable skill in bushcraft first aid but

comes with responsibilities. Proper technique, sterilization, and aftercare are paramount to ensure the best possible outcome for wound healing in the wilderness.

Managing Severe Allergic Reactions

In the wilderness, where medical help may be hours or even days away, it's crucial to understand how to manage severe allergic reactions, also known as anaphylaxis. Anaphylaxis is a rapid, life-threatening allergic response that requires immediate action. This guide will help you identify and manage severe allergic reactions in a bushcraft setting.

Recognizing the signs and symptoms of anaphylaxis is the first step in managing it. These can vary but often include difficulty breathing, swelling of the face, lips, or tongue, hives, abdominal pain, vomiting, diarrhea, a sense of impending doom, and loss of consciousness. The onset can be swift, developing within seconds or minutes of exposure to the allergen, which could be anything from insect stings to food.

Upon recognizing the signs of anaphylaxis, immediate action is necessary. Quickly assess the environment's safety for both the responder and the victim, ensuring no ongoing exposure to the allergen.

Send someone to call for emergency medical services immediately. In remote locations, this may involve signaling for help or using a communication device if one is available.

If the individual has a history of severe allergies, they may carry an epinephrine auto-injector (EpiPen). Administering epinephrine promptly can be life-saving. Familiarize yourself with the instructions for using an auto-injector before you find yourself in an emergency. Remove the auto-injector cap, place the injector against the person's thigh, through clothing if necessary, press firmly until the injector activates, then hold in place for the recommended duration (usually about 10 seconds). Remove the injector and massage the injection site for 10 seconds to enhance absorption.

After administering epinephrine, lay the person flat on their back with their legs elevated to improve blood flow. If breathing is difficult, help them sit up to make breathing easier. If vomiting occurs, turn them on their side to prevent choking. Keep a close eye on the person's breathing and consciousness. If they stop breathing or if their heart stops, be prepared to perform CPR immediately.

Shock can make a person feel cold, so cover them with a blanket or extra layers to help maintain body heat. If symptoms do not improve within 5 to 15 minutes, and you have access to a second epinephrine auto-injector, administer a second dose following the same procedure as the first.

Monitor the person closely once the immediate threat has passed, as anaphylactic reactions can recur, necessitating further treatment. When help arrives, provide a complete account of the incident, including the trigger (if known), the time and dose of epinephrine administered, and any changes in the person's condition.

Prevention is a critical component of managing severe allergic reactions. If you or someone in your group has known allergies, take proactive steps to avoid exposure to known allergens. Carry appropriate medications, including at least two epinephrine auto-injectors, and ensure that everyone in the group knows how to use them.

Understanding and preparing for severe allergic reactions in the wilderness can mean the difference between life and death. You can save a life by recognizing the signs of anaphylaxis, acting quickly to administer first aid, and seeking professional medical help as soon as possible.

Field Management of Dental Emergencies

In the wilderness, where professional dental care is not immediately accessible, managing dental emergencies effectively becomes crucial. This section delves into practical strategies and techniques for addressing common dental issues that may arise in bushcraft scenarios. Understanding these methods can significantly alleviate discomfort and prevent complications until professional help can be sought.

Various factors, including decay, abscess, fracture, or a lost filling, can cause toothaches. When a toothache occurs, it's essential to rinse the mouth with warm water to clean it and gently use dental floss to remove any food caught between the teeth. If swelling is present, applying a cold compress to the outside of the cheek can offer some relief. It's imperative to avoid placing aspirin or any other painkiller against the gums near the aching tooth, as it may burn the gum tissue. If the pain persists, consider using clove oil (eugenol), which can be applied to the affected tooth or cavity to reduce pain.

If a tooth is broken, chipped, or fractured, rinse the mouth with warm water to clean the area and apply a cold compress to the face to reduce swelling. If the break is minor and there's no pain, it's still important to be cautious about chewing or applying pressure to the affected tooth. For more severe breaks causing pain, temporary dental cement can be applied, if available, to protect the tooth until professional care can be accessed.

A knocked-out tooth presents a dental emergency that requires quick action. One should hold the tooth by the crown (the part usually exposed in the mouth) and rinse off the root of the tooth in water if it's dirty, avoiding scrubbing or removing any attached tissue fragments. Try to reinsert it into the socket gently. If that's not feasible, place the tooth in a small milk container (or water if milk is unavailable) to keep it moist. It's crucial to seek dental assistance as soon as possible since the chances of saving the tooth decrease significantly as time passes.

Sugarless gum can be used as a temporary measure for a lost filling. Chew a piece of gum and then use it to cover the cavity, ensuring it's sugarless to avoid causing pain. For a lost crown, attempt to slip it back over the tooth if it is still intact, coating the inner surface with dental cement, toothpaste, or denture adhesive to help hold the crown in place until professional dental care can be obtained.

An abscess is an infection that occurs around the root of a tooth or in the space between the teeth and gums. Abscesses are severe conditions that can damage tissue and surrounding teeth, with the infection possibly spreading to other parts of the body if left untreated. If an abscess is suspected, seeking professional dental care is vital. In the meantime, rinsing the mouth with a mild saltwater solution several times daily can help draw the pus to the surface and relieve pressure.

While these techniques provide temporary relief and can be crucial in managing dental emergencies in the wilderness, they do not replace the need for professional dental care. It's essential to seek out a dentist as soon as possible to address the underlying issues and receive appropriate treatment. Prevention is always better than cure, so maintaining good oral hygiene practices, even in the wilderness, is critical to avoiding dental emergencies.

Handling Psychological First Aid

In the wilderness, where the unpredictability of nature meets the fragility of the human condition, psychological first aid becomes as crucial as treating physical injuries. This section delves into the nuanced approach required to administer psychological first aid in bushcraft scenarios, emphasizing the importance of recognizing and addressing mental health crises that may arise from high-stress situations.

Psychological first aid in the wilderness begins with establishing safety and security. The first step is ensuring that all individuals involved in a bushcraft expedition are physically safe. Once physical safety is secured, attention must be turned to creating a sense of psychological safety. This involves reassuring individuals, providing accurate information about the situation, and setting realistic expectations for rescue or self-recovery.

Communication plays a pivotal role in psychological first aid. Active listening, without judgment, allows individuals to express their fears, frustrations, and concerns. It's essential to validate these feelings, acknowledging the stress and fear as normal reactions to an abnormal situation. Simple, clear, and calm communication can help reduce anxiety and provide comfort and stability.

Orientation to the present is another critical component. Individuals experiencing acute stress may become disoriented, confused, or overwhelmed by their thoughts. Gently guiding them to focus on the here and now through mindfulness techniques or simple sensory exercises (such as naming objects they can see, hear, or touch), can help mitigate panic and ground them in reality.

In situations where trauma has occurred, it's crucial to avoid forcing individuals to recount their experiences before they are ready. Instead, offer support and let them know that their reactions are normal and that seeking help is okay. Encourage, but do not pressure, them to share their feelings and experiences at their own pace.

Building community and support among the group can also aid in psychological recovery. Encouraging teamwork, shared responsibilities, and mutual support can foster a sense of belonging and collective resilience. This communal approach can be efficient in bushcraft settings, where reliance on one another is often necessary for survival.

Finally, it's essential to recognize when professional help is needed. Signs that someone may need more than basic psychological first aid include persistent disorientation, severe anxiety or panic attacks, uncontrollable emotions, or thoughts of self-harm. Planning for evacuation or establishing communication with emergency services for psychological support becomes a priority in these cases.

As we transition from addressing immediate psychological needs to considering the longer-term care and planning necessary for recovery, it's clear that psychological first aid is not a one-time intervention but the beginning of a continuous process of support and healing. The skills and principles outlined here are vital for the immediate aftermath of a crisis and the ongoing journey back to normalcy and health.

Evacuation and Long-Term Care Planning

Understanding evacuation principles and long-term care planning is crucial in the wilderness, where professional medical help may be hours or even days away. This knowledge ensures the well-being of the injured and prepares the group for potential challenges during the evacuation process. The aim is to equip you with the necessary skills and knowledge to plan and execute an evacuation effectively and manage long-term care when immediate evacuation isn't possible.

Evacuation planning starts with assessing the injured individual's condition to determine the necessity of evacuation. If the person's life is in danger and cannot be stabilized on-site, evacuation becomes a priority. However, evacuation in the wilderness is complex. It requires careful planning, considering factors such as terrain, weather conditions, the physical condition of the injured, and the distance to the nearest medical facility.

Communication is vital; always carry a means to communicate with emergency services, such as a satellite phone, a personal locator beacon (PLB), or a two-way radio. Before embarking on your journey, inform someone outside your group about your plans and expected return time.

Depending on the terrain and the condition of the injured, evacuation methods can range from manual carries and makeshift stretchers to water transport or even air evacuation if the situation is dire and resources allow.

It's also crucial that at least one group member is proficient in navigation, equipped with detailed maps of the area, a compass, and a GPS device to mark your location and the best route to reach help or guide rescuers to your location.

When evacuation is not immediately possible, providing long-term care becomes essential. This involves creating a stable environment for the injured, monitoring their condition, and administering first aid. Protect the injured from the elements by setting up a shelter and using insulation materials to maintain their body temperature, preventing hypothermia or heatstroke, depending on the weather conditions.

If the injured can eat, keep them hydrated and provide them with energy-dense foods to maintain their strength and aid recovery. Regularly monitor and tend to their injuries, including cleaning wounds, applying fresh bandages, and managing pain while being vigilant for signs of infection or deterioration in their condition.

The mental and emotional state of the injured can significantly impact their physical recovery, so offer constant reassurance, keep them informed about the situation, and engage them in decisions about their care to maintain their spirits.

Keep detailed notes of the injured person's condition, the care provided, and any changes over time, as this information can be invaluable to rescuers or medical professionals when they take over.

In conclusion, being prepared with evacuation and long-term care planning skills is essential, even though the hope is that you'll never need to use them. The wilderness is unpredictable, and knowing how to manage serious injuries can make the difference between life and death. The goal is to stabilize the injured and get them to professional medical care as safely and quickly as possible.

Chapter Summary

- Suturing is a critical skill for managing deep wounds in the wilderness, requiring proper assessment, sterilization, and technique.
- Suturing is suitable for clean, sharp cuts but not for puncture wounds, animal bites, or infected injuries due to the risk of trapping bacteria.
- A suture kit should include sterile needles, thread, scissors, forceps, and antiseptic solution; improvisation requires prioritizing sterilization.
- The suturing process involves threading the needle, using forceps to align wound edges, and spacing stitches for optimal healing. It also involves close monitoring for infection signs.
- Managing severe allergic reactions (anaphylaxis) in the wilderness involves recognizing symptoms, administering epinephrine, and ensuring the victim is warm and monitored.
- Dental emergencies in remote areas can be temporarily managed by rinsing, cold

compresses, temporary dental cement, or reinserting a knocked-out tooth into the socket.
- Psychological first aid focuses on establishing safety, active listening, orientation to the present, and recognizing when professional help is needed.
- Evacuation and long-term care planning in the wilderness require assessing the need for evacuation, communication with emergency services, and providing shelter, hydration, nutrition, and psychological support.

THE JOURNEY AHEAD

A thunderstorm in the wilderness.

Reflecting on What We've Learned

As we pause to reflect on the wealth of knowledge we've amassed throughout our exploration of bushcraft first aid, we must recognize the profound impact this learning can have on our outdoor experiences. The journey from understanding the basics to mastering advanced first aid techniques has equipped us with the skills to respond to emergencies and instilled in us a more profound respect for the natural world and the unpredictability it harbors.

The progression from foundational principles to complex interventions has been deliberate, ensuring that each step builds on the last, reinforcing our competence and confidence. We've learned to assess situations with a critical eye, apply our skills under pressure, and adapt to the challenges presented by remote environments. These are not just lessons in first aid but in resilience, preparation, and the importance of maintaining a calm, focused mindset in the face of adversity.

Our exploration has spanned a broad spectrum of scenarios, from managing minor injuries that can be treated on the spot to addressing life-threatening emergencies that require immediate action and evacuation. We've delved into the intricacies of wound care and fracture management and the critical steps to take in the event of bites, stings, and exposure to the elements. Each topic has been approached with a practical, hands-on perspective, emphasizing the importance of practice and repetition in ingraining these skills into our muscle memory.

However, the acquisition of knowledge is only the beginning. The actual test of our learning lies in its application — not just in emergencies but in our everyday approach to safety, risk assessment, and how we prepare for our adventures. It's about integrating these principles into our planning, ensuring we have the necessary supplies, and making informed decisions about our activities and the environments we choose to explore.

As we move forward, it's crucial to remember that the field of first aid, particularly within the context of bushcraft and wilderness settings, is ever-evolving. New techniques, research findings, and technologies continually shape our understanding of best practices. Staying informed, seeking further education, and practicing our skills regularly are essential steps in ensuring we remain prepared to face whatever challenges the wilderness may present.

In embracing the journey of continuous learning and improvement, we enhance our safety and well-being and contribute to the safety and well-being of those with whom we share our outdoor adventures. The knowledge we carry into the wilderness is a powerful tool that empowers us to face the uncertainties of the natural world with confidence and competence. As we look ahead, let us commit to maintaining our curiosity, seeking new growth opportunities, and upholding the highest standards of safety and preparedness in our bushcraft endeavors.

Continuing Education in Bushcraft First Aid

Now, the importance of continuous learning in bushcraft first aid cannot be overstated. The wilderness is ever-changing, and so are the techniques and knowledge necessary to ensure safety and well-being in these environments. This section aims to guide you in engaging in ongoing education in bushcraft first aid, ensuring that your skills remain sharp and your knowledge up to date.

First and foremost, it's crucial to recognize that learning is a lifelong journey. The completion of a bushcraft first aid course is just the beginning. The real test of your knowledge and skills comes when you're faced with real-life situations that demand quick thinking and decisive action. Commit to regular review sessions of your first aid materials to prepare for these moments. This could mean monthly refreshers on specific techniques or quarterly reviews of your first aid knowledge base. The goal is to keep the information fresh in your mind so you can easily recall it when needed.

Another key aspect of continuing education is staying abreast of new developments in first aid and wilderness medicine. Medical advice and best practices evolve as new research emerges and techniques are refined. Subscribing to relevant journals, joining professional organizations, and participating in forums dedicated to wilderness first aid are excellent ways to ensure you're always informed about the latest advancements.

Practical experience is also invaluable. Seek opportunities to practice your skills in controlled environments, such as workshops, simulations, and training exercises organized by bushcraft schools or outdoor clubs. These experiences reinforce your existing knowledge and expose you to scenarios you might not have considered before, broadening your understanding and capabilities.

Networking with other bushcraft enthusiasts and first aid practitioners is another beneficial strategy. Sharing experiences and knowledge with peers can reveal insights and tips you might not find in textbooks or formal courses. Moreover, building a network of like-minded individuals creates a support system that you can turn to for advice or assistance when faced with challenging situations.

Finally, consider advancing your education through additional certifications or courses that delve deeper into specific areas of wilderness medicine. Specialized training in trauma care, search and rescue operations, or herbal medicine can significantly enhance your ability to provide adequate first aid in the bushcraft context. These courses expand your skill set and increase your confidence in handling a more comprehensive range of medical emergencies.

In conclusion, the journey of learning in bushcraft first aid is ongoing. By embracing continuous education, staying informed about new developments, gaining practical experience, networking with peers, and pursuing advanced training, you can ensure that you are always prepared to provide competent and effective first aid in the wilderness. Remember, the goal is not just to be ready for emergencies but to prevent them from happening in the first place. Through diligent study and practice, you can achieve this goal and enjoy safer, more rewarding adventures in the great outdoors.

Building a Community of Preparedness

It now becomes increasingly clear that the path to actual preparedness is one we walk with others. The knowledge and skills we acquire, particularly in the realm of first aid, hold the potential to safeguard our own lives and fortify the well-being of those around us. In this spirit, building a preparedness community emerges as a pivotal next step in our collective journey.

The essence of such a community lies in the shared commitment to learning, practicing, and teaching the fundamentals of bushcraft first aid. It's about creating a network of individuals who are equipped to handle emergencies in the wild and passionate about passing on this critical knowledge. This endeavor begins with each of us as we take the initiative to reach out, connect, and engage with fellow enthusiasts through local clubs, online forums, or educational workshops.

Organizing regular meet-ups, whether in person or virtually, can be a powerful platform for exchanging ideas, experiences, and best practices. These gatherings offer invaluable opportunities for hands-on learning, where members can demonstrate first-aid techniques, share insights on navigating medical emergencies in remote settings, and discuss the latest advancements in wilderness medicine. Such interactive sessions reinforce our skills and strengthen the community's bonds, fostering a sense of camaraderie and mutual support.

Moreover, collaboration with local emergency responders and wilderness medicine professionals can elevate the community's knowledge base to new heights. Inviting experts to lead seminars or workshops enriches the learning experience. It bridges the gap between bushcraft enthusiasts and the broader medical community. These partnerships can facilitate access to advanced training, resources, and certifications, further empowering individuals to make a meaningful difference in emergencies.

In fostering a community of preparedness, we also embrace the responsibility of advocacy. Raising awareness about the importance of first aid in wilderness settings, advocating for accessible education, and supporting conservation efforts are all integral to our mission. By championing these causes, we contribute to the safety and well-being of our community and the preservation of the natural environments we cherish.

As we look to the future, let us remember that the strength of our community lies in its diversity, inclusivity, and shared dedication to learning and growth. By coming together, we can create a resilient network of bushcraft practitioners ready to face the challenges of the wilderness with confidence and competence. In doing so, we ensure our own safety and uphold our commitment to the ethical exploration and stewardship of the natural world.

The Ethical Wilderness Explorer

As we journey through the wilderness, embracing bushcraft skills and the essentials of first aid, it becomes imperative to reflect on the broader impact of our adventures. The wilderness is not merely a backdrop for our endeavors but a living, breathing entity that demands respect and ethical consideration. As ethical wilderness explorers, our responsibilities extend beyond personal safety and survival; they encompass a profound respect for the natural environment and a commitment to preserving it for future generations.

The concept of Leave No Trace is foundational to ethical wilderness exploration. This principle guides us to minimize our impact on the natural environment, ensuring that we leave the wilderness as pristine as we found it, if not in better condition. Practicing Leave No Trace involves simple yet impactful actions such as packing out all trash, including biodegradable materials, staying on designated trails to prevent erosion, and setting up campsites at least 200 feet from water sources to protect aquatic ecosystems.

Moreover, ethical wilderness exploration involves understanding and respecting wildlife. This means maintaining a safe distance from animals, not feeding wildlife, and securing food and trash to avoid attracting animals to campsites. Such practices protect the animals and their habitats and ensure the safety of explorers.

Another aspect of being an ethical wilderness explorer is the commitment to sustainable resource use. This includes using renewable resources, such as fallen wood for firewood instead of cutting live trees, and relying on a camp stove when firewood is scarce or when fires are prohibited due to the risk of wildfires. Water sources should be treated with care, using biodegradable soap sparingly and well away from them to prevent contamination.

In bushcraft first aid, ethical wilderness exploration takes on an additional dimension. It involves not only being prepared to address our own emergencies but also being willing to assist others in distress while ensuring that our interventions do not further harm the environment. For instance, when constructing a stretcher from natural materials, choose abundant and renewable materials and ensure that your actions do not unnecessarily damage the surrounding flora.

Finally, being an ethical wilderness explorer means advocating for protecting and preserving natural spaces. This can involve participating in conservation efforts, supporting policies that protect the environment, and educating others about the importance of ethical wilderness exploration.

As we embrace the wilderness with confidence and respect, let us carry the principles of ethical wilderness exploration. By doing so, we ensure that the beauty and majesty of the natural world remain accessible and intact for those who follow in our footsteps. The journey ahead is not just about mastering the skills of bushcraft and first aid; it is about becoming stewards of the wilderness, safeguarding its wonders for the future.

Embracing the Wilderness with Confidence and Respect

We now arrive at a pivotal moment of reflection and anticipation. The wilderness, with its untamed beauty and inherent risks, beckons us to step forward with a blend of confidence and respect. This journey, enriched by the lessons of ethical exploration and the practical skills of first aid, equips us to embrace the wilderness not as conquerors but as humble guests.

Confidence in the wilderness is not born solely from mastering survival techniques or memorizing first aid procedures. It is cultivated through a deep understanding of our environment and physical and mental capabilities. This confidence is a quiet assurance, a readiness to face challenges without underestimating the forces of nature. It is knowing how to respond to a snake bite as much as recognizing when to turn back because the risks outweigh the rewards. Confidence is also in the acceptance that, despite our preparations, the wilderness will always hold the unexpected. It teaches us to be adaptable, to use our knowledge creatively, and to trust in our ability to navigate the unknown.

Respect for the wilderness is the other half of this symbiotic relationship. It acknowledges that we are part of a larger ecosystem, with responsibilities towards its preservation. Respect is shown in our actions, from minimizing our environmental impact to understanding the significance of the flora and fauna we encounter. It recognizes that the wilderness does not bend to our will and that our survival and enjoyment of it depend on our willingness to learn from it and adapt to its conditions. Respect is also in our preparedness to handle